BLACK MAN IN THE CIA

An Autobiography

by

Leutrell M. Osborne, Sr.

Editor: Gary Revel

Book Design: Gary Revel

Published by: Jongleur Music Book Publishing

Cover Design: Gary Revel

ISBN-13: 978-1468195361

ISBN-10: 1468195360

Note from the Publisher:
Last minute requirements by the CIA to delete or change some terms and phrases due to recent CIA policy changes have been made prior to publication. The changes were incorporated in rewrites or simply made by deleting the term and/or phrases in question and in it's/their place using the word, OMITTED.

Dedication

I dedicate my story to my mother, Ella , my wife of over 52 years Rose Marie and those who already know the truth but for various reasons have not done anything about rectifying the injustices that continue to prevail in our Espionage Enterprise (EE).

Rose Osborne

65 Year Birthday Celebration for a Virtuous Woman

TABLE OF CONTENTS

PREFACE

The Black Man In The CIA (BMCIA) provides insights into growing up in Washington DC and working for one of the 17 Departments and Agencies of the National Intelligence Communities in particular, the Central Intelligence Agency (CIA) during the Cold War years. Leutrell M. Osborne Sr. (Mike) tells his story to document the former Spy Manager's history in the CIA while providing insights for others to understand his rise to become a spy manager supervising CIA agents and assets in over 30 countries, and in addition to that also becoming the only spy manager who also has gained six years of experience in Information Assurance (IA). Leutrell is also the Chief Visionary Officer (CVO) for The Dark Operatives Series.

Chapter 1:

Spy Dreams (1939-1957)

On September 12, 2001, the day after the infamous 9/11 Attack on the United States of America, Black Entertainment Television (BET) scheduled me to appear on national television to discuss "The Attack on America." I appeared with California's Democrat Congresswoman, Maxine Waters, who is one of my favorite members of the House of Representatives. This appearance on BET was my first exposure to a global audience by transnational mass media, but not the last.

While awaiting the twenty-minute limousine ride to BET headquarters from the upper Northwest Washington D.C. home of our third daughter, Natasha Inez Osborne, I considered my unique position. My childhood dreams came flowing back as if a curtain were going up on precious memories.

I had wanted to be a "spy manager" since I was twelve years old. The yearning to be a "spy," was strong and only later did I learn the Central Intelligence Agency (CIA) Case Officers are really more like spy managers because they supervise many agents. That wishful twelve-year-old could never have imagined what his future would hold; becoming a pioneering CIA African-American spy manager, rising within the ranks from CIA clerical employee, to Case Officer, and

1

mentoring others through that system. As unlikely as it seemed, my vision became my reality.

Now, I was going on national television, as an authority, to analyze the possible causes and aftermath of the nation's most devastating national security breaches. We all know 9/11 was an unprecedented act of catastrophic terrorism in the United States and we still feel the repercussions. At that moment, we were still reeling from the shock and I was no exception despite my background in counter-terrorism which is part of Counter Intelligence (CI). The impact on the World Trade Center and Pentagon became metaphors for the deeper impact on society. It led to a shift in national priorities.

Considering my upcoming interview and looking deeply within myself. I pondered, "Who am I this time on planet Earth? What is my karmic relationship with the CIA?" The answer resonated from the depths of my being – "A Spirit in human form." I had always been spiritual but in that instant I realized how much more important that inner strength would be after an event such as 9/11, not only for myself but our whole culture.

As my life flashed before my inner eye in rapid review, it appeared that everything had fallen into place in my life. Everything was clicking or going as intended – from my rewarding family-life, to meeting my personal and career goals, to growing in spiritual faith and action. I always hoped to be an inspiration to others. I had realized long ago that fulfillment is a key to well-being. I've heard that called "self-actualizing." I have always been an action-oriented person. What I envision I put into action.

I pondered the important roles of the two women who mean the most to me because they helped shape who I am: my wife, Rose Marie

Battle Osborne and my mother Ella, who happened to have been employed at CIA in my youth. She was my inspiration and first mentor.

My mother enabled me to be born as Leutrell Michael Carlton Osborne, Sr., also known professionally as "Mike" Osborne inside the CIA for over 26 years. My wife Rose accompanied me through my experiences at the CIA and assisted me in accomplishing my dream of public service in the intelligence community. I was and continue to be a successful Counter Intelligence (CI) expert and most of all an "investigator" and "fixer."

My life is a quest. I remain a seeker, and now I create my own "missions," which I feel serve my community and the world at large. Certain issues are recurrent themes of interest. As a former "Cold Warrior," I remain committed to freedom, truth and justice.

Now what was my set up? It was ordained by my Higher Power on who would become my mother and father thus providing the DNA, cultural and ethnic set up. My mother--Ella Grisby Motley and my biological father--William Mason Osborne provided the DNA for the confidence, characteristics and skills I needed to grow up in Washington D.C. as a light skinned Black man. Although I shared his genetics, I did not meet my father, William, until 1960 at the age of twenty-one. Therefore, I did not get parental nurturing from him as a youth. There also was no record of my father on my birth certificate. In addition, two months before I was born, he and his wife just had a baby child -- my half-brother, William Osborne, Jr.

My birth record states that my mother was 19 years old and gave birth to me at Women's Hospital near Georgetown, Washington, D.C. She had to interrupt two years of education at Virginia State College in order to usher me into this world. Ella essentially prepared me for life before she died at the relatively young age of forty-one. She encouraged me to strive, have confidence in my potential, and to actively apply myself toward my desires with deliberateness. One might say she guided me in the Law of Deliberation Creation (LDC) way before the LDC was described and practiced. My experience confirmed that what you put your energy into, what you think and focus on, grows. I still operate by that principle; remaining open to potential in myself and others.

On the day that I was born, July 8, 1939, global attention was focused on an unusual spy story. That day, the front page of the New York Times reported that German spies had infiltrated Romania while working undercover as clowns in a German circus on tour. The fake clowns were exposed as a result of a counter-spy operation conducted by the Romanians. Eventually, the headline "German Circus Clowns Spies, Romanians Report" was depicted in a James Bond movie. The film storyline of "Octopussy" presented spies dressed as clowns in one of its more dramatic undercover scenes. When Bond dresses as a clown to escape German police, we are reminded in the clandestine realm, things are never what they seem. Intelligence works under deep cover and assumes many disguises.

Some people believe in "signs." Perhaps something can be discovered about a person's personality and destiny by reading the lead story and headlines printed in the newspaper on the day that an individual is born. Observing the breaking news on the day of my birth, one could say that "spy vibes" were in the air when I emerged from the womb. Some may even say that I was destined to become involved in the world of espionage, to live that double life.

In The Hero With 1000 Faces, Joseph Campbell describes the myth of the "hero," which embodies the adventurous journey of self-discovery each of us experiences throughout life's passages. The hero's journey is the template of most successful stories and films. It is a story

4

of transformation. The hero is "called" to adventure and that adventure is his or her vocation. As Campbell rightly predicts, "once having traversed the threshold, the hero moves into a dream landscape of curiously fluid, ambiguous forms, where he must survive a succession of trials." That describes my entry into the clandestine service. Both challenges and unexpected rewards waited for me on the unknown path. I became a "transformation agent."

Like myself, the so-called hero often has a very improbable beginning. Mother Ella named me using her maiden name, when I was born: Leutrell Grisby. Just before I entered the Kindergarten at Morgan Elementary School in Washington, D.C., I insisted my mother change my name to my father's surname, Osborne. My only explanation for such an action at that early age was that I knew by having my father's name Osborne the question of my being born out of wedlock would not always surface.

My name then became Leutrell Carlton Osborne. When I was christened in the Roman Catholic Church, the church named me Michael. My mother, who formerly was a Methodist, converted to Catholicism before I was seven years old. To the best of my knowledge my mother's deep study of world religions enabled her to select Roman Catholic as her religion. Thus, her being Catholic and my being baptized Catholic as a child enabled me to get my middle name Michael. So eventually Leutrell Michael Carlton Osborne, Sr. became and is my full name.

Ella Grisby was what some of us call a strong "sista" mother who was most of all, a very independent woman and a very nurturing mother. She was born in Washington, D.C. on January 1, 1920, so she was about 19 years old when I was born. She was the daughter of William Henry Grisby from Spencerville, Maryland, and Olivet Van Der Lippe who died shortly after she was born.

My grandfather's family came from the plantations near Fredericksburg, Virginia and my great-grandmother was a Geechee from Charleston, South Carolina. The Geechee or the Gullah is African Americans found in the Sea Islands of South Carolina and Georgia who have roots in Sierra Leone, Africa. Willie Grisby was the son of Mahala Ross, from Fredericksburg, Virginia, and George Grisby, a coachman from Spencerville, Maryland.

As I was growing up in Washington, D.C., my mother, Ella, urged me not to search for my biological father, William Mason Osborne. Over the years, I eventually learned that my biological father, whom I resembled, was a light-skinned Negro who was born on October 28, 1915 in Clearfield, Pennsylvania. Some might say that my father was actually a mulatto, a hybrid of European and African descent. We eventually learned that my father's birth was the result of a mixed marriage between Alice Russell and John Porter Osborne. My father, William lived and worked in Washington most of my early years, but our paths never crossed.

Alice Russell, my fraternal grandmother was a light-skinned African American who was allegedly a Quaker. John Porter Osborne was descended from Europeans. My mother felt I would not gain much from being in contact with my biological father; instead, my maternal grandfather, Willie Grisby served as my surrogate father. One day when I was a teenager, Granddaddy Grisby told me that he had once run my father William out of town because he was hanging around the Spencerville home trying to see my mother. With an absent father and being my mother's first child, I was the "little man" of the house. I was the king of house and the only child of Ella. But after her marriage to my step-father, Frank Motley, Jr., family life began to change rapidly. I eventually became her eldest of five children. In 1946, my mother married a dual trumpeter, Frank Motley from Cheraw, South Carolina. Frank had been educated at South Carolina State

College as an engineer. However, he defied his parents' wishes and pursued a profession as a musician. Frank met my mother in Washington, D.C. while renting a room in a rooming house owned by William and Lillie Mae Woods next door to where my mother lived with her Aunt Sarah Richardson at 2434 Ontario Road, N.W.

My first Motley sibling, Frank the III was born in 1946 in Chicago, Illinois. Even at seven years old, my inclination was to help my mother in raising my siblings. Even after my mother returned to Washington with my brother, I still did not know any of my Osborne relatives. I definitely identified only with my mother's family and eventually my Motley siblings from the union of Ella and Frank Motley, Jr. They eventually had four children, two boys and two girls: Frank III, Victoria Lillian, Francine Hadaway and Thomas John.

When I was twelve years old, we were living in Ledroit Park in Washington, D.C. at 82 V Street, N.W. when I first began dreaming and thinking about working for the CIA. At that time in 1952, my mother Ella was working at the CIA as an overt employee -- a clerk in the National Photographic Intelligence Center (NPIC). Some years later, I met some of her former co-workers who worked in the NPIC, which is now The National Geo-Spatial Intelligence Agency (NGA).

In hindsight, I think that many of my conversations with Mother must have centered on photography. Somehow it stuck and I gravitated toward it consciously and unconsciously. I even taught myself the fundamentals of the photographic art, including how to develop and print pictures in my basement when we lived in North East at 313 44th Street in Deanwood. With this skill, I would have something to offer the Agency when I applied. At that time, my view of the CIA was no different than my view of Superman, the Green Hornet, Batman and Captain Video. I thought super heroes constantly in the midst of adventure worked for the Agency. Little did I know my heroic fantasy would become my reality.

I went to segregated D.C. public schools up through the 10th grade. Segregation (which created a fictional paradigm of "Separate But Equal" schools) was abolished in 1954, three years before my graduation from Roosevelt High School in Washington. I did have one year at Dunbar High School in Washington, D.C., which set the stage for my participation in high school cadets. This was very important in my development as an impressionable young man. To continue answering the question "Who am I?," I offer the fact that my mother had nurtured me to be super inquisitive and investigative in my thinking while I was still a child, and well before I got the notion to be a "spy manager." Not ever seeing or even knowing much about my biological father until after I was 21 years old did have a serious effect on me. Because he was absent, I realized that his only direct influence on me was the DNA I had inherited from him. My mother's nurturing and guidance through my early years greatly contributed to my character, personality and tenacity, creating a drive to achieve and make something out of myself even before she died. Looking back now I am sure that the DNA from my biological parents provided me the confidence, characteristics and skills I needed to grow up in Washington D.C. as a light-skinned Negro without much money.

"If only my mother could see me now," I mused, still awaiting my BET interview. I contemplated the struggle within lifelong personal experiences and ambitions and the hard-won actualization of my dreams. As Leutrell Michael Carlton Osborne, Sr., known professionally as "Mike" Osborne, I had accomplished my vision of public service in the CIA as a Counter Intelligence Officer.

1952

My mother Ella worked in the federal government near the Lincoln Memorial, in temporary buildings that most people thought belonged to the Navy Department, however, the temporary buildings also housed employees of the CIA. I do not remember when my mother began working there but know that it was only a short time after I had young sisters at home in 1951. I began to get the idea that I should get that good government job at the CIA like my mother. She had begun working there shortly after she returned to Washington and we were living at 82 V Street, N.W. I would stress that my mother did not talk much her work nor did I get too much information from her, but it was enough for me to get the idea to seek similar employment and my mother groomed me with guidance on how to get hired. She had ended her employment at CIA by 1957 when I got hired out of high school.

Ella's dream required her to nurture and train me so that I gained extra-ordinary knowledge on the workings of the United States government and other governments. Her traits, talents and skills which she acquired from her parents, enabled her to accomplish her mission and destiny of grooming children who would continue her legacy of healing people. In looking back at myself and my siblings born to Ella, I would say the five of us tend to serve others and help them solve problems in life which I interpret as "healing others." Ella Grisby's personality was shaped in such a way that she gave birth to children who helped change the world's perception of Black people--especially in the Intelligence Community. That is part of what I was able to do at

CIA. Historically, she and I were to become the first Black mother-son duo in the CIA.

A former CIA director once described the Enterprise of Espionage (EE) as the "Great Game." My involvement began at the periphery via conversations at the kitchen table with my mother. By age twelve, I had a clear understanding that she worked for a government agency that was important, secretive and often dangerous and I wanted to emulate her. It became quite clear that she was part of a vital federal government operation that was always in the midst of important and often very controversial activities intended to help the United States stay safe in the midst of extremely dangerous foreign threats. I, too, deeply desired to serve. I felt the "call." As time passed, my destiny became unavoidably clear.

Another factor in my mother's diligence to educate me was that she had only one kidney. In retrospect I believe she knew she would not live to see me reach all of my goals in the Agency. She nurtured me with tons of knowledge and leadership skills to help me succeed. She was very patient in preparing me to learn skills that would make me attractive to the Agency. Her preparation of me was so acute that by the age of 12 all I could imagine myself doing as an adult was becoming a spy for my country, regardless of the danger that might involve. Mother likewise ensured that I knew about world religions and politics and we would often talk for days about both subjects. These talks continued until my hormones started raging as a teenager and I became more interested in chasing girls than the pursuit of learning from her wisdom and experience.

My mother's mission was to birth children who would change the world's perception of Black people in the National Intelligence Community. For the record the National Intelligence Community includes the CIA and the Department of Justice. As I said, my mother and I are the first CIA mother and son duo. My brothers Thomas and Frank obtained law degrees and have flourished as attorneys. She and two of her sons are the first Black mother and son duos employed by two agencies the Intelligence Community. Thomas J. Motley became an influential U. S. Department of Justice Assistant U.S. Attorney and now is a D.C. Superior Court judge. The other son, Frank Motley, Jr. helped design the curriculum for many Indiana Law students who have eventually worked their way into the Intelligence Community. Frank continues to be at the Law School at the University of Indiana.

While she was "just" a clerk in the early days of the National Photographic Intelligence Collection (NPIC), where images from overhead photography were analyzed, she never actively encouraged me specifically to study, learn and do photography.

I initially was the "little man" of the house and remained so as the eldest of her five children. Living in Washington D.C. with my Great Aunt Sarah Richardson and Grandfather William H. Grisby, at 2434 Ontario Road, once my mother had left the CIA and would go on the road with my step-father Frank as he performed as a musician, I viewed the 'little man' responsibility as a vital family necessity..

In the midst of all this I continued to think of myself as one who was destined to become a "spy" for my glorious Untied States of America. It is most interesting to me now that I kept the spy dreams to myself. I didn't even tell my best friend Sonny Floyd Short until many years later when I recommended that he too get a good government job at CIA.

My view of the CIA as the headquarters of superheroes didn't become acutely realistic to me until I was in high school. It was then that I realized I could launch a career in espionage by developing my talents as a still photographer. Still, the CIA didn't become a truly

11

tangible reality until I applied for and got the job; then entered CIA training. That's when the reality of it all raised its head and hit me right in the eye. There's nothing in the world like CIA intelligence training for a reality check but that wouldn't come to full completion in me until 10 years later.

My great aunt Sarah was a registered nurse and my grandfather Willie was a government worker and paper hanger at night. He taught me to hang paper and I earned extra money helping him. I learned even more about life by being with him because he had many friends all over the city and he would also take me on his night jobs.

The Grisby family, headed by my great-great Grandfather John Grisby, owned two acres of land in Spencerville, Maryland. Granddaddy Willie and I would go there almost every weekend to feed the chickens and horses and generally take care of them. I once told him how I was going to buy a certain house I had seen while we were on our way out to the country. It was on Alaska Avenue where no Blacks lived. He knew what I had said was out-of-the-box thinking and said, "Boy, your mind works overtime, doesn't it?!" That's what he used to say, usually after I had told him about some new thought or vision that had popped into my head.

One day I told him that I would someday have a large family with lots of children. I told him I did not want my children to grow up without companionship.

"MMMmmmm, that is a new one on me, son," he responded. "I don't know quite what to say about that. You keep thinking and I'll catch up to you one day. Just don't wait for me because you are already in a family and you are only eight years old--but keep thinking up new ideas and dreaming new dreams. You're going to grow up to be quite a young man."

I knew little about the romance of mother and biological father, but on one of our trips my grandfather did tell me he chased my father William down a country road near the farm in Spencerville, MD. one day -- pointing a shotgun at him. Obviously, my father had gotten into trouble because he was already married to another woman when I was conceived. I never heard my mother ever say that she loved William Osborne. She let me know who my father was with no additional information. She often reminded me not to look him up or to get in contact with him because it would be more detrimental to me than to him. On the other hand, William Osborne was a compulsive man.

From my direct contact with him, I did not observe any desirable family-oriented or fatherly traits, nor any particular traits I desired. I did not respect him on the family side of the ledger. One might say his family and fathering skills were practically worthless. However, I did inherit the characteristics and talents that enabled me to become a spy master. He had a personality that pleased the women and even was able to flatter Rose, especially one time when she wasn't feeling too well. He washed the dishes and brought her coffee while she was still in bed. He was good at doing thoughtful things that won over the other person.

He was the product of marriage between Alice, a light skinned Black woman, and a white man named John Porter Osborne. Yes, my grandfather was a white man. He and my fraternal grandmother were from Lewistown, Pennsylvania where mixed marriage was lawful. It didn't last, according to my father, William. John Porter Osborne divorced and moved to Clearwater, Florida. My efforts to find my fraternal grandfather in Florida failed to reveal any information.

My maternal grandfather William Grisby was probably the first to notice my mental gifts. Later, a friend, who was an astrology buff, wrote about me after doing my astrological chart just for fun: "There's little that you aren't capable of intellectually, for you have a quick mind and remarkable memory."

Time and time again throughout my life, I would rely on those gifts, especially when competing against others who were more prepared to take on various challenges. I worked hard in school and enjoyed math and science. My English was not the best. I would much rather talk and converse. I can do that for hours and hours at a time. As an extrovert, I enjoy telling stories and sharing insight. I also love to create illusions by saying certain things in certain ways and changing my behavior to suit each occasion. So, there is a bit of an actor in me, too. Such a talent serves a CIA intelligence professional well.

My mother Ella was the first to notice the actor in me and she nurtured it. I remember I told her I was going out for a part in the school play when I was in the third grade. My mother asked how I thought I was going to get the role. I told her I could remember the lines, out-talk the other classmates, and show-off, so I knew I would get the part.

Mother always took time to talk to me whenever I had something on my mind. She made me feel very secure and loved. When she wasn't available, my grandfather always seemed to be there to fill in. Talking to these elders about everything from school to girls to puberty to God, gave my mind a workout regularly. To this day, I think of them when interacting with my children and grandchildren.

It seems as if my life has gone according to a script or a dream with my mother's spirit there to help inspire me to keep my dreams alive. In essence, her spirit has provided my drive.

I generally explain that my Spirit collaborated with my Higher Power so that I would be born to Ella and William. The story, as I heard it, was that the family home at 2434 Ontario Road, NW, Washington, D.C. was uniquely situated so that my mother Ella Grisby could be with two men in her life -- William and Frank. In 1938 William Osborne's wife's family, the Fenwicks, lived next door on the North side of 2434. Because of this geographic location and other reasons my father had an opportunity to spot and eventually entice my mother -- who was all of eighteen years old.

My life at 8 years old with a step-father

In 1946 and 1947, Frank "Dual Trumpet" Motley, an itinerant musician, from Cheraw, South Carolina, roomed with the William Woods family on Ontario Road in the house on the South side of 2434. And guess what? Right, Frank met Ella and eventually married her in 1946. Ella was twenty-five years old by then. They gave birth to four children--two boys and two girls, Frank Jr., Victoria Lillian, Francine Hadaway, and Thomas John. Frank had a hard life as a traveling musician, struggling for 25 years to keep himself and six other musicians employed in the music business. He had his bouts with compulsive behavior and I pledged never to be like him. I made my mind up to out-perform him as a father, a husband and as a provider. I guess one might say that both would be father figures in my life. My paternal father and step-father both inspired me to be a better father and husband than I perceived them to be.

I was seven when my mother married the well-traveled Motley. I guess my mother knew she would have to abandon me to pursue her own dreams. After all, she was a young woman and the man who became my stepfather swept her off her feet and took her on the road with him.

While my mother traveled with Frank, I was nurtured and raised by my great aunt, Sarah Richardson, a registered nurse, and my

15

grandfather, Willie, as the family called him. He was a government worker by day and a paper hanger by night. Since he taught me to hang paper, I earned extra money helping him. He had friends all over the city and he introduced me to them on his wallpaper hanging night jobs.

At age 13, I was transferred to Shaw Jr. High in the 7th grade; we called it 7b then. I even met Hank Aaron who visited Shaw.

I lived at 82 Vee Street NW with the Motleys. Sister Victoria came. Around that time Ella went to work for the CIA. I then went to Langley Jr. High School for the 7th and 8th Grades while we lived in NE. We lived at Aunt Julia's house. She rented to us when I attended high school at Dunbar, the first year. For the record, I left all Black schools and desegregated Roosevelt High School in the 11th and 12th Grade. Maybe that later gave me courage to move into the culture of CIA.

About this time I began also accepting the belief that I suffered from the "marginal man syndrome." I acted out and demonstrated this syndrome in my earlier years. During high school I had to fight to survive. I was nurtured in high school believing that I did not fit in one group that was Black nor in another that was white. I happened to be light skinned and had real challenges accepting myself. I cursed my father who was light skin and blamed my mother for not falling in love with a Black man who was darker. In hindsight, I may have argued the other way, but I was solid in my understanding that I was culturally and ethnically Black. If I had any doubts, my grandfather William Henry Grisby who was my father figure and Black as an ace of spades left no doubt where I belonged and who I was. He loved me wholeheartedly. He lived next door in a rooming house.

To accomplish this super human mission, my mother Ella worked for the CIA but continued preparing me for my destiny. She taught me about world affairs. She equipped me with people skills. I practiced talking and exchanging information with my mother and family members. My mother ensured herself that I was able to think on my feet and use my cultural experiences and understanding of people to propel myself over four continents in CIA's super secret spy directorate, clandestine services, for over 25 years. My compassion for others, and capacity to find solutions and form effective teams went beyond my employment with CIA. I am proud to say I became one of the Who's Who in Black procurement and minority business.

My mother encouraged more wholesome thinking as well as ensured that I had a vision with a purpose to achieve what I wanted. My mother, who realized her medical condition meant a shortened lifespan, showered me, her oldest son, with the skills and abilities that enabled me to take care of my own family. In hindsight she also equipped me to be able to assist in raising my two brothers and sisters when needed. I grew up fast and seemed to always be "a little adult" with exceptional people skills. My mother knew I inherited a lot of my father's relationship skills and she made sure I used them in a positive way. She held my father in contempt because she objected to his use and abuse of people, especially woman. She did not want me to look for him but after she died in 1960 when I was 21 years old I found him.

The Marginal Man

One day I was challenged to do something really awesome. Understand that in my mind I did not see myself as a white person nor as a person who could pass for white because my thinking was Black, period. I had never tried to pass myself off as White. So when my friends dared me to walk into the White Only entrance of the movie theater and sit in the White section, I did not look at it from the skin color perspective. I was Black and thought Black and it was simply unheard of in those days for a Black person to sit in the White part of the movie theater. Jim Crow was alive and well in the United States, especially Washington, D.C., the capital.

I took them up on the challenge. I truly believed that I could do anything. Indeed, I thought that by going through that door and acting like I belonged in the best section of the theater, I would prove something to others and myself as well. As I strode into the theater and took a seat in the White Only section, my friends just looked at me and laughed. They couldn't believe what they were witnessing. Since I won the bet, after the movie they paid up: they all pitched in and treated me to an ice cream cone. It had worked. With that attitude and my fair complexion, I had breezed right past the doorman, who smiled at me and gently nodded as if he knew me or thought he knew my father or mother.

What a crock! Discrimination in America. What a crock! But for the color of skin, the worst white people in the world could get in and the best Black people could be kept out.

We lived in Capital View NE, Washington, D.C. Then Capital View was an upper class new community for Black people.

I believe I cultivated my gift for gab as a result of the vast social contact that my grandfather forced upon me. I enjoyed being around him, his friends and his fellow paper hangers. I never was around any Black man who did not work at least two jobs, thus I had plenty of role models during my early years. The image of men working hard would help shape my self-image and work ethic. Time and again throughout my life, I would rely on those gifts.

I relished taking responsibility for the household and making my mother's life as manageable as possible. I washed floors, cooked and helped raise my younger siblings. My mother's conversations with me from birth developed within me keen listening and critical thinking skills. She never talked to me as if I were a child. I was her little man as soon as the maternity room nurse placed me in her hands at the hospital. I would become her student on world affairs and world religions. Since she knew that she was not going to be around for the long run, she needed me to grow up and act as a mature person as soon as possible.

During my early years, my mother made sure that I had no fear of failure and encouraged me to perform above expectations. At 7 years of age I had a newspaper route in my neighborhood and as a teen I went to Atlantic City, New Jersey to work and experience more of life. I still had the chore of helping to raise my brothers and sisters from my mother's marriage to Frank Motley, Jr., the musician. Later on my mother would bless my loving wife Rose Marie Battle with her approval and welcome her into our family; then with Rose at my side, I was able to exceed everyone's expectation in family and government service.

I had already begun living in accordance with my conscience because the CIA hired me after high school as a still photographer. My days of hard work under the mentor-ship of my mother in the dark room paid off. She enabled me to develop a skill that was immediately valuable in the working world and in developing as a CIA Case Officer. I immediately gained friends, allies and mentors. I call these mentors "godmothers" and "godfathers." These mentors augmented the guidance that my mother gave me and I set my sails to become more than my mother ever imagined.

I enjoyed Dunbar High school, a D.C. Black institution and became a cadet in the school's junior ROTC program. Most cities did not have a cadet program tradition like D.C. I made the most of it. At

Dunbar, I learned to march with rhythm. I later went to Roosevelt High school the next year after the schools were desegregated. I continued as an enthusiastic cadet at Roosevelt. Roosevelt was a mixed cultural environment with a thick white veneer. I liked cadets and the military. After the 11th grade I took the examination for becoming a high school cadet officer. After the fact, I learned that I had scored the highest on the military examination but was given the lowest rank.

I didn't quite know this had happened but I knew that I was good at what I did. I was co-Captain of the Roosevelt drill team, a lieutenant in the cadet corps and the company. I was in Company G, and we won the school competitive competition but lost in the city-wide competition. It was this competition that re-kindled my belief that I had learned to march with rhythm at Dunbar. However, the military instructor at Roosevelt, Captain Gaison had prevented me from teaching this to the company at Roosevelt. I truly believe had I been allowed to do that, we at Roosevelt may have won the city-wide high school competition in 1957. I am sorry that some others can't seem to learn to march with rhythm. In short, I suspect that is why Mr. Gaison wouldn't let me teach the cadets how to do it. In retrospect, this was one of the first realities for me that another could stand in the way of my ideas and suggestions for improvement. My fate would adversely be controlled by someone without my vision and definitely not operating from the same paradigm.

My high school was desegregated but we could not have a prom because Whites and Blacks could not dance and socialize together. At least, this was the prevailing attitude of the principal. In those turbulent late 50's at a desegregated D.C. high school that's how it was. I was one of the few who dared transfer from a Black school to help in the process of desegregation of the American public school system. Still, those of us who dared do this and suffer the consequences of discrimination are fortunate people. Many of us discovered that the events were a state of mind and I used the experiences later in handling other discriminatory actions in the workplace.

Attending the desegregated and formerly all-white high school, Theodore Roosevelt, enabled me to develop self-confidence, specifically, in dealing with non-Blacks and other cultural groups. I used this strongly developed confidence throughout my life, and applied it as a transformation agent.

The severely restrictive "Jim Crow" system had conditioned Blacks to act in a non-threatening and "socially acceptable" manner to non-African Americans and to show submission. My desegregated high school experience helped me overcome the inclination to put on the invisible chains of Black self-effacement.

When I reached high school, I realized that I could actually become a spy manager and use my talents as a still photographer to advance up the ranks, just as my mother said I could. When I was seventeen years old, I did not understand that a spy was technically an agent employed to obtain secrets and what I really wanted to become was a spy manager. I later learned in the CIA that my ultimate goal was to become a Case Officer (C/O) who directs and manages CIA agents and assets. Once my dream was focused, I vividly imagined myself in that role.

1954 Supreme Court School Desegregation Decision

The Supreme Court Decision desegregating public schools (Topeka vs. Board of Education) did away with the social lie that schools were separate and equal. In hindsight the Black schools in the District of Columbia were not equal; in many ways, to me, they were better than the White schools in Washington, D.C. However, I am glad desegregation did come because it enabled me to convince myself that I had just as much going as any white person. The 1954 The Supreme Court decision impacted me directly by the opportunity to transfer from a Black high school, Dunbar, to a formerly all white DC High School, Roosevelt. Like many other Blacks with high IQ's I transferred to participate in D.C.'s grand experiment. For me that experiment never ended.

I wasn't one to keep my big ideas to myself. I told my buddies in the neighborhood about my dreams. I would come up with grand scenarios for games we played. It wasn't just cowboys and Indians, it was secret agents and nuclear bomb threats. It was the United States vs. the Russians.

Roosevelt proved to be a pivotal place in my life, because that's where I cultivated my relationship with my high school sweetheart, Rose. About 18 months after we met, we were married; we eloped. We now have five children and eight grandchildren. Of course, if Rose's mother had had anything to do with it, none of them would have been born, because she hated the idea of me marrying her sweet and tender daughter. Mrs. Inez Battle did everything she possibly could to stop me, but I was too brash and too much in love to be denied.

Classmates from Roosevelt were destined for success. James Lancaster, Jr., Russell Miller, and James Collins were three of them who were cadets with me. Charlene Drew Jarvis was another. She was in Rose's class, a year behind me.

I went to Roosevelt because it was close to home on Delafield Place. I opted to take Chemistry when I was in the 10th grade and still wanted to take biology as a Senior before I graduated. As fate would have it, I took the second semester in biology from the same teacher that had Rose in another period. She knew we were dating and permitted us to work on a science fair project together. We built a model of the uvula, which is the organ that absorbs nutrients into the blood that flows through the body.

I was not so fortunate the second semester of biology. I had another biology instructor, Ms. Owens, who had a physical impairment that caused her to use the back of the chair for support as she scooted around the room. I had a significant incident when all students were assigned a presentation on the life cycle of a frog. I took it upon myself to go to Howard University, a university in Washington D.C., and get a college textbook to use for my presentation. When I gave it, the instructor said "You made a mistake" and she explained my mistake. I waited until after class to defend my presentation. I knew the rules of discrimination: that is, Blacks are never right when a white person told them they were wrong. Also, at the time, I knew the principal made sure the students didn't socialize with each other. Anyway, the teacher gave me an F for the class at the term break and a D in deportment because I challenged her. It was quite a bump in the road because I was suspended from the Cadets as a result.

By my late teens, my life consisted of two passions one, my wife Rose Marie, and the other, chasing the CIA spy manager position that I eventually secured. Rose and I married on September 9, 1957 and the CIA hired me on October 14, 1957. I tell everyone, "Just imagine, at 17 years old I had two passions, Rose and the CIA," and I landed them both. What I envisioned was enough for me to win my wife and get the entry-level job at CIA to begin the process of becoming a spy master in the Espionage Enterprise (EE).

Earlier that year in May, I was interviewed by the Central Intelligence Agency while I was still in Roosevelt High School. I was hired through one of the former traditional employment methods used

23

in 1957. Personnel recruiters came to a Washington D.C. high school, in my case to Theodore Roosevelt High School, and gave three applicants a clerical test.

Later I would discover that two of my Roosevelt High School classmates were also hired by the Agency. I was the only Black. The others were a Jewish fellow and a female named Helen Zirnite. The male, Robert Anthony Kogok, was known simply as Bob. Helen achieved her objective and became a secretary at the CIA for a few years and lived long enough to play a significant role in my life as well. She was helpful to me in securing an assignment in the Far Northern Country (FNC) in 1963. Bob had wanted to become a dentist but ended up in the Agency along with me and Helen.

We were some sort of early Rainbow Coalition. Little did I know that the Civil Rights Movement was about to kick into high gear. Little did I know that I would, in my own way, overcome many of the disadvantages of cultural discrimination within the bowels of the government's most enigmatic and culturally-biased institution.

One thing I did know: As long as Rose was by my side, I knew I could do anything. One year earlier, wanting to get my military service obligation out of the way I had joined the D.C. Air National Guard. I had just started the 11th grade at Roosevelt High School. Some of the people I met while in the Guard were friends, or became friends, who remained so even to the present: Vaughn Phillips, a D.C. Guard air traffic controller and Frank Hogan, Jr. worked in Crypto with me. Eventually, Frank married my best friend's sister, Catherine Short. They divorced after having three children. Dewey Holmes was also in Crypto with me in the DC National Guard. He was married to Savannah, one of the most memorable NCIOs and another was a member of the John Birch Society. For this writing let's just say his name was Bennett. One the other members of the DC ANG was a

24

genuine CIA communicator but continues under official cover. I knew the CIA had the same type of communications protocols that I was doing in the DC ANG.

My experience with the Air National Guard also instilled and reinforced certain values in me, including the desire for patriotic service. In the Guard I had the opportunity to find more male role models and saw others work their way up the chain of command. The Guard "initiated" me, and I made the passage into manhood. I became an adult.

As a teen, I profiled the girls. I interviewed them about their hopes and dreams. I actually kept notes on file cards in a little black file box. She wouldn't know she was being interviewed, of course. I wanted to know what her aspirations were, what her family plans were and, most importantly, how many children she wanted.

I wanted a large and loving family. During my interviews with these girlfriends, I made a mental note of the size of their hips. My mother had told me that wide hips indicated that a woman's pelvic area would be amenable to child birth. I eventually honed in on four girlfriends with wide hips who later married and gave birth to a total of 22 children. I was almost a year older than Rose. The night that I met her was the night before I was scheduled to leave town to go to Atlantic City for a summer job. I convinced her and her sister, Peggy, to pick me up the following morning at my house and take me and my luggage to the bus terminal. During that summer, I wrote Rose about 25 letters. I was sure enough in love with that woman. She and I both wanted a life of adventure and we would later have just that. Heck, the adventure started at the end of the following summer, when I asked her to marry me and she agreed, against her mother's wishes.

My thoughts never strayed far from her though circumstances kept us apart. When the long, hot summer ended in 1956, I could not wait to return to Washington, so I could court my sweetheart, Rose. I never doubted the strength and power of our love. I had distinct and compelling sense of destiny about our relationship. Something deep in me was convinced we were meant to share our lives, and so it has been. We couldn't remain apart. Though Rose was one year behind me in school, we impulsively eloped and married in Rockville, Maryland. During the interim, I had to amend my CIA security paper work. Our elopement, marriage and family were important to me. The elopement and our actual living together were challenging but we adapted and thrived. I still knew I'd be hired. Rose graduated the next year from evening school. After all, we now had one another and we were waiting for me to get my good government job.

Ours was a happy, quaint life in the nation's Capital. By the following summer, I was ready for something new to happen. I was biting at the bit to get on with my career in government service. Then, on one sunny day in September 1957, my lovely bride handed me a letter from the CIA. The letter was my duty notification that requested me to report to work as a GS-3, step one civil servant earning $3,870.00 a year. I would be a CIA still photographer.

Rose was so excited that I was finally getting that "good government job" that we ran four blocks from Allison Street NW Washington, D.C. to Delafield Place to tell my mother, Ella. We all were happy now I could leave that one dollar an hour job at the haberdashery. I had been recruited by the CIA through one of the traditional methods employed in 1956.

Fate had helped me meet and fall in love with Rose the night before leaving for Atlantic City, and we began our mutual adventure that we continue to enjoy. Rose was my top choice. She gave me six wonderful children.

The Elopement: MARRIAGE

Our elopement, marriage, and family were important to both of us. I had asked Rose to marry me many times before she finally accepted. I remember clearly the night she stopped refusing my proposal. One Saturday, about a week before Labor Day in 1957, she and I were supposed to join my buddy, Vincent and his girlfriend, Melvoid for a drive-in movie. When Rose asked her mother for permission to go to the drive in, for some reason, her mother instituted an unreasonable curfew.

"You can go, but be back by 10 o'clock tonight," she said.

Her mother was simply trying to interfere with our love affair. She was trying to protect Rose from the inevitable. Rose and I were determined to be together and as rebellious teenagers, her mother's attempt to place barriers between us only irritated us.

When Rose told me about the curfew, I was livid. The movie doesn't even start until nine!

"Your mother just doesn't want us to be together." Seizing this opportunity to convince her to be my wife, I, hugged her tightly and added: "If you were my wife, your mother couldn't tell you what to do and when to do it." Finishing my smooth rap (which to this day she fondly calls "the unbelievable rap"), I kissed her and whispered into her ear: "We could go to the movie and stay as long as we wanted to, plus we could do whatever else we wanted to do whenever we wanted to do it. Just marry me, baby."

"Okay, that's it. Let's do it, sweetheart," Rose replied. "Take me away from this prison!"

I didn't bother to ask Mrs. Battle for Rose's hand in marriage. I knew her answer would be a loud and resounding, "NO!" So, I convinced Rose to elope.

I did my research and worked out a plan. I arranged everything. I discovered that we would be able to get married in Rockville, Maryland, if my mother signed a consent form for me and Rose fudged her age. My mother signed and Rose said she was 18. We obtained the marriage license from the courthouse and prepared for a civil service, because the Catholic church would not permit us to get married in the church. We found a minister who agreed to marry us. The quick and simple ceremony was held in the living room of his house September 9th, 1957, the day after Labor Day.

Vincent and Melvoid who were not married became best man and maid of honor. My mother, Ella, did not attend, but thank God she signed the papers for me the week before.

After marrying me on Monday, Tuesday, September 10, Rose went to school and I went and got her. That evening Helen, her sister, came to my house to make an appeal.

Tuesday was a cooling off day... and as surely as the world turned, the wheels were turning in my head. By the next day, I had some solid ideas to bring my wife and I together -- at last. I figured that Rose's mother was really trying to say, "No job, no place to live, no way. I gotta break this up!" So, I decided: I would get a job, a place to stay and -- Voila! Rose and I would get together.

Wednesday, September 11, 1957 I met the Minister and took on the challenge. Thursday, September 12, 1957 I had the job that day and re-visited the Minister. That evening things started to break. I drove Vincent's car up to Rose' house Friday September 13th. My new mother-in-law Inez did not recognize Friday as the beginning of the weekend however this would be the day that would turn into the beginning of the rest of our lives spent together as family.

Chapter 2:

The ABC's of the CIA

We lived a happy, quaint life in the Nation's Capital. Like many young people, I was not really aware of my social and economic shortcomings. One might say, I was oblivious to the low status of my family's economic standing and that was definitely below the poverty level. However, I was chafing at the bit to get a job in government service. Rose and I were sharing that humble room one block from my mother's house at 1309 Delafield Place, when "lightning" struck. I was accepted into the CIA.

My entrance on duty took place in two phases: Phase one was the first day when I entered the Agency pool where people who did not have a clearance were assigned temporarily. Phase two came when I actually entered into the Directorate of Operations after my clearance was approved.

Therefore when I first reported for duty at the CIA, I was assigned to the Agency pool pending completion of the background processing. At that time, the Agency site was on 16th Street, NW, curiously just one block from the Soviet Embassy. I didn't care where I was placed. All I knew was that I was making a "big salary" and didn't have to work as hard as I had been working at the clothing store, where I had been the stock clerk and janitor. At the pool, we hardly worked at all. As a matter of fact, we played "match pack football" several hours a day. Match pack football was a little game people played flicking books of matches through the index and baby fingers of other people's hands. It was a silly game, but it sure killed time while we awaited further assignments.

I met Joe Hornet during that time. Both of us were young, eager and right out of high school. We both were "feeling our Cheerios," as they said back then, and thus, we hit it off well -- at least during working hours and lunchtime. One might also say we "clicked" or felt like brothers.

During my stay in the pool, which lasted about two months, not one other Black person entered the pool. I didn't pay too much attention to this because my experience from then until now confirms Blacks tend to distrust working in or around what is perceived to be "the law." Also going overseas is not a high priority agenda for most Blacks. By the way, the CIA is not a law enforcement Agency but that is another conversation when one is discussing aspects of cultures. Also some of my friends have challenged my insights and generalizations like this, but it is my own point of view – what I call my "tude" or attitude.

Still, a part of my intent in telling my story is to encourage others who are fearful to venture and seek employment in the Agency and other secret government organizations. The description below of the culture in the CIA in 1957 best sets the stage for understanding the cultural barriers that Blacks faced and many like me over came. However, before I actually get into the story, let me deal with another subject that I have confronted throughout my entire life.

Living in the USA as a light skinned Black man enabled me to experience what some of us call the "light skin" Negro experience. I have to get deep into our cultural mindset and ask you to imagine that there are two types of Black experiences, depending solely on the perceptions of others. In one, the person knows without doubt who they are as far as a cultural identity. In the other, especially for those

31

with multicultural roots, there are conflicting messages both internally and from the environment. There are periods where the person does not know who they are and must grow toward an understanding of their core self, their essential being. If you can buy into these two paradigms, maybe you can understand my experiences in life, from the inside out, before and during my CIA employment.

In simple language, yes, I had an advantage, because at first glance, the mere sight of me may not trigger others into their biases. However, in subsequent experiences, it didn't matter whether I looked Black or not because the culture in the CIA, without doubt, enabled one to quickly learn who had the advantages and who didn't.

Blacks in the CIA were looked upon as "people at risk." The CIA was no different than any other U.S. federal institution. It, too, was a "plantation" in 1957 when I arrived. Thus, other Blacks saw its few Black employees as so-called "slave" employees. I am elaborating the distinction because I personally believe that I am a descendant of "stolen people." My African ancestors were obviously victims of an institution called "slavery," so to me slavery means a state of mind that tends to become inter-generational. I use the phrase "stolen people" to counter the use of the term 'slaves' and to characterize the true heritage of the people from Africa who suffered in the institution of slavery that is unique to the cultural experience in the USA. In my mind's eye, slavery is a state of mind and the stolen people did not have to accept the concept or mindset even though they suffered the penalties of the institution.

Clearly, CIA management did believe that the Black employees were no different than the stolen people who were formerly on the plantation. The top leadership in the Agency was non-Black, even though a few other Blacks like me were employed in the bowels of the Agency.

Overseer-like supervisors and senior managers played the role of "masters" and wreaked havoc among Black employees. Yet, the Black CIA employees had much more freedom, independence and autonomy than most Blacks employed elsewhere in government. Consequently, we did not have to be infantile or abjectly docile in order to be trusted and effective. Still, we were limited. We did not make the decisions about anyone's future. We were expected to be submissive. We were viewed as a people who had no influence in their work, just cogs in a wheel.

In the midst of the social, political and professional dynamics, some of the supervisors took an interest in me and helped me understand the inherent plantation mentality within the Agency. Some of my mentors even helped me overcome the barriers of this plantation. I call these mentors "godfathers and godmothers."

The character and nature of the CIA can be interpreted by the names of the components and the names of the Agency itself. When I joined the CIA in 1957 and began working in the Directorate of Operations (DO), I learned that it had just changed the DO's name from the Directorate of Plans and Propaganda (DPP). The DO was also called the Clandestine Services (CS) in part because this directorate as compared to the other three is where the more "secret" things took place. I even got used to being called a DO spook. Therefore, personnel in the DO performed the real sensitive intelligence work collecting information and directing CIA agents and assets. The key point is that CIA personnel do 'intelligence" work and are not law enforcement personnel. This significant activity called intelligence work is very different in nature than law enforcement work and is one major distinction between the CIA and the FBI. As I get into the details on the Espionage Enterprise (EE), especially on the EE activities of the Federal Bureau of Investigation (FBI), I'll set the stage in the way things used to be.

The CIA performed EE operations abroad and when operating in the US, such activities were generally coordinated with the FBI. The FBI performed internal security and protected the USA and US citizens. That is called internal security and such activities included law enforcement similar to the police. In short the FBI locked people up and the CIA did not have such powers nor did we learn to lock people up. When needed to operate abroad, the FBI performed under the coordination of the CIA Station Chief.

Remember that the CIA performed intelligence operations while the FBI performed law enforcement activities. For those of us in the intelligence business, there is a very large and distinct difference. I found out that CIA Case Officers were not able to retire and get the benefits like FBI Special Agents (SA) since they retired under US laws related to law enforcement. I just happened to learn that tidbit way before I quit because I wanted to know how CIA retirement worked and how I could use my 26 years service in the federal government as a part of my retirement.

When I traveled on public transportation to and from work, I would wait for the Agency shuttle bus at CIA headquarters on E Street N.W. near the Department of State. We then rode the shuttle bus to the "tempo" buildings.

The Agency headquarters building was located at 2430 E Street, N.W., not too far from the Lincoln Monument's Reflecting Pool. World War II temporary buildings had been constructed on the mall near the Reflecting Pool. I worked in 'L Building' for a few years until the new Headquarters building was constructed in Langley, Virginia. In the temporary buildings, the workers in the Clandestine Service (CS) were separated from the overt employees who were at the main Headquarters Building on E Street.

CIA Director Allen Dulles' chauffeured limousine would pass by me while I waited for the shuttle. I made it my business to look for his long black vehicle. The trappings of official federal power intrigued me. I would ride the public bus to the Department of State, which was located across the street from 2430 E Street, and I would then walk up the hill to the main entrance. As Dulles' limo passed CIA headquarters, I would often see him smoking his pipe and reading the morning newspaper.

I felt closer, yet still far away from my dream position. The Agency was established ten years before I was hired. I realized early on that I would not become a Case Officer working as a Still Photographer in the Microfilm Section of the CIA's Clandestine Services Records Integration Division. My vision and intent was still a more influential position.

By this time, I had acquired a great deal of insight into the ABCs of CIA. I knew that I did want to become a Case Officer. The genuine meaning of a Case Officer really began to take hold of me and I began making job moves so that I could get where I wanted to be. Even at that early stage of my development in the CIA, I knew that there were no such things as "operatives," even though that type of wording was used in military settings, movies, novels and newspapers. For some reason, they could not bring themselves to simply call these people plain old Case Officers, managing, directing and leading agents, most often in foreign environments. Of course, there are exceptions to where and how Case Officers operate.

I like to say that I would have made the perfect spy, but in actuality, I never became a spy, per se. I became a successful Case Officer and spy manager in the CIA's DO. By being a CIA Case Officer employed in the DO as we called it, I was also known as an Operations Officer. Have you got it yet? A spy manager is also called a Case Officer (C/O) and an Operations Officer because of the work we do which is supervising CIA agents, spies and assets. While I was doing spy manager work, most people in the Agency, knew me by my professional name, "Mike" Osborne.

My title as an operations officer is similar but definitely not the same, as the audience sees in James Bond movies. That is, Bond is a conglomerate of both the Case Officer and the agent into one being, whereas this is not the true nature of a Case Officer. Operations officers are best termed Case Officers because we supervise and lead CIA agents and assets. Now this term Case Officer has evolved into the more colorful term, "spy master." It helps make the point that the Case Officer is a leader of humans who acquire information that the US Government wants to know but the adversary attempts to actively protect and prevent from getting into the hands of the US Government.

The job of a Case Officer or spy manger is considered to be one of the most responsible positions in the CIA. A Case Officer in the CIA is my preferred term for members of the Clandestine Service (CS), who supervised CIA agents and assets. For me, this thinking coincides with that of former Director William Colby's aspiration for an American Intelligence Service. Case Officers differ from Special Agents (SAs) of the Federal Bureau of Investigations (FBI) in that Case Officers are not part of the legal authority of the government that performs law enforcement even though both supervise spies and assets of the federal government. Case Officers have more authority and power in leading people and managing things designed to achieve objectives of U.S. foreign policy based on "National Security interests".

Let me make another very important distinction between Case Officers and many other US Government personnel operating in the National Intelligence Community. One has to ask the question, "Is the CIA's Directorate of Operations, where the Case Officers are located, a part of the law enforcement mechanism in the US Government or not?" The distinction becomes clear if one attempts to retire and collect as a member of the US Government's law enforcement establishment. CIA Case Officers don't qualify for the entitlement because Case Officers are not law enforcement. You can do your own research, but I find this clarification useful especially in today's changing intelligence climate where law enforcement and intelligence are merging and can be confusing to some.

My world inside the Agency had changed as our family started to grow. On August 3, 1958, the day after we moved from the apartment on 13th Street to 636 Webster Street in Northwest, De Levay, Cabina Osborne our eldest daughter was born. Rose settled in as a mother and wife while I focused on executing the steps in the CIA that would help me achieve my objective to become a spy manager. The next year, our second daughter, Monique Therese Osborne, was born on August 22, 1959 while I was away at Lackland AFB, in San Antonio Texas, attending Air Force cryptographic training. By then we had moved from our home at 636 Webster Street, NW, via my mother's home on 5th Street to our own home at 5724 Eastern Ave. NE, Washington, D.C. Our family was off to a great start.

Cold Warriors

The Cold War was "frozen over" when I joined the Agency in 1957. We, the people of the United States, knew who the enemy was: Russia -- the Soviet Union and its Communist satellites. The major Eastern European countries were our rivals. Since the Soviet Union was our adversary, I obtained significant knowledge about the country during my early years in the Agency and harbored an ambition to "recruit" a Soviet spy. Primary targets were members of the Soviet intelligence services, scientists and diplomats.

Let me elaborate just a little, especially since I said we knew who the enemy was. The Cold War period involved espionage between the United States and the Soviet Union, the Peoples Republic of China (PRC) and Cuba. When people of my period refer to espionage, we are talking about spying among these countries.

Now for the history and irony. I had joined the DCANG during my 11th grade at Roosevelt High School in 1956 because I wanted to get my military obligation out of the way in six years. The end result of this extraordinary sacrifice in later years at CIA turned into an exceptional serendipity.

While in San Antonio, Texas at the crypto school I learned the art and science of cryptography, the science of creating code and decoding encrypted code. We moved within the year and I went off to D.C. Air National Guard technical school at Lackland, AFB, Texas. I was in "crypto," which later proved to be a phenomenal asset. I had to position this information on my cryptographic operations because I was deep into my DC Air National service since I knew I had to do my six years so I could get overseas. In other words, the Agency wanted employees to have no military obligation. While I was still in RID and deciding to get overseas, I realized that I had the necessary qualifications to get a job in CIA's Office of Communications.

It's very interesting that the RID mail room job that I did on the evening shift so I could go to college helped me learn world geography, including the names of places around the world. Just imagine that the Agency mail went to just about every place around the world. I easily began knowing the places that I might get to visit and work in one day. Of course that was my belief then. Actually what happened was I used my crypto capability to seek a position in the Office of Communications (OC). Knowing that one of the supervisors who was assigned in the DCANG had gained legitimate employment in the OC inspired me.

So I went straight for the jugular and asked for an assignment. To my surprise and dismay I was rejected. It had nothing to do with qualifications. Yep, you guess it -- in 1960 the Office of Communication had a policy of not accepting "Negroes." I was told bluntly, (ironically by a person named Bob White), "We don't hire Negroes in Commo." Man, I jumped all the way back into my Roosevelt High School days when I had my run in with my biology teacher. Those old feelings of rejection and hurt were rekindled. So I went back to my job in the mail room, but I still nurtured my dream.

In 1959 I was a Staff Sergeant in the D.C. Air National Guard (DCANG), and had been stationed for eight weeks at cryptographic school training attending Air Force cryptographic training. I had secured military leave from the Agency so I could attend Air Force training at Lackland Air Force Base, San Antonio, Texas. So with this history and irony, you get to connect the dots of history and the beginning of my information assurance and transformation agent connectivity; then, almost like a miracle, I got a call with a request for an interview because one of the European Branches wanted someone for a mailroom position. Oh, was I elated! This was just what I really wanted but naturally there were challenges. I had to terminate day school and hope that I could get classes at DC Teachers College at night so I could continue my education. Thus, I made a transition into an operating division as well as eventually qualifying for my first overseas assignment. My entire position, mail and pouch work enabled me to move from the bowels in the RID of the organization where I began learning the ABC's of CIA to an operating branch mail room working for Ms. Dottie Tyson. It is at this point of my education that I realized that I got my PHD in Espionage Enterprise (EE) before my undergraduate degree. By the way the EE included the enlightenment in the Agency operation known as Covert Action operation.

After I met Mr. Big Post, who was then the Chief of the CA Division, I began really understanding the game of intelligence way before I got into the Career Training Program (CTP). What caught my attention was that the Agency began changing terminologies. Thus, by 1959, I had acquired military and Agency security training. As a crypto operator in the DC Air National Guard I had US Air Force security training. Then I received Agency security training. About this time the intelligence terms I had learned began changing.

The Agency was formed in 1947. Covert Action intelligence operations were, at the time, called Propaganda Operations and were under the direction of the National Security Council (NSC). A carefully phrased "catchall" clause, [Section 102(d)(5)] stated, "the CIA shall perform such other functions and duties related to intelligence affecting the national security as the National Security Council may from time to time direct. I took this to mean that Clark Clifford (1906-1998), (friend and confidante to Presidents Truman, Kennedy, Johnson, and Carter), believed that Covert Action intelligence operations were not mentioned specifically and that they would be separate and distinct from the normal activities of the NSC. He expected them to be limited in scope and purpose - thus the import of limiting language "affecting national security.."

Propaganda Operations changed the name to Propaganda and Plans (P&P). Then it eventually became known by its current name: Covert Action (CA) intelligence. To familiarize the reader with the craft of espionage or the espionage enterprise, let me outline three espionage operations and comment on the various differences in operations conducted by different members of the National Intelligence. I am including some examples and evidence that will enable us to note what has happened over the years, stressing the shifts from CIA dominance and control of certain types of operations in

National Intelligence. In the current situation, other agencies now control and run them, especially the U.S. Department of Defense.

I met Mother Hope*- when I began working in the European Division at Headquarters. Mother Hope turned out to be one of my favorite people because she treated me like a son and she was like an adopted mother for me. When I met her, she was working in the European Division mail room as a mail clerk. She entered my life in 1959. I now consider her one of my first Agency "godmothers," since she mentored me like her adopted child. My job in the Branch mail room required me to collect the Branch mail from the Division's mail room. I had natural reason to contact and visit with mother Hope. Given the fact that the Division mail room personnel separated the mail for the various branches, Mother Hope and I often had lots of contact on a regular basis. We became very close at work and outside of work. After Mother Hope passed on, I continued contact with her two daughters, Barbara and Hope who are both near my age. I even became the godfather of Mother Hope's two grandchildren, Maria and Jay Chisolm, who are Barbara's children. Mother Hope and I had regular discussions on many topics. Besides what mothers and sons talk about, she pointed me toward the right people who further enlightened me.

When Mother Hope introduced me to Mr. Big Post I began learning in earnest about Covert Action (CA) intelligence operations. I also call them "dirty tricks." Many people recall the term from the days of Watergate. The official term for CA is just an intellectual word game but in the street "dirty tricks" is a more explicit description of what goes on.

Mr. Big Post eventually became a very important "godfather" and instructor for some of my early lessons in Covet Action intelligence of the EE.

1963

The opportunities and methods I developed provided further insight into how successful tactics can be used to achieve spectacular results. My personal story became one in which the CIA eventually chose to deploy my whole family overseas.

Soon after I got my job in the European Branch mail room, I met someone from the European Division who enabled me to learn about being a CIA Case Officer specializing in Counter Intelligence. Merwin Peake, aka Mountaintop, happened to be the Chief of CI unit in one of the European Branches. As such, Peake was responsible for countering espionage by the Soviet Union and other adversaries of the United States.

Let me make a serious conceptual point here about definitions in the Espionage Enterprise (EE). Note I said Peake countered adversarial activities. When nation states perform intelligence they do the same as the US in performing three types of intelligence activities: foreign intelligence collection (FI), counter intelligence (CI) and Covert Action (CA) intelligence operations. It is the latter that tends to confuse the public and I want to ensure that in my story there is no confusion. So if Mr. Peake countered terrorists, I am referring to terrorists as secret para-military personnel who are also called adversaries in my lexicon.

CIA and the FBI today both perform operations to neutralize and eliminate intelligence operations of adversary forces which under most circumstances refer to nation-state intelligence organizations that perform those three types of intelligence operations: FI, CI and CA operations. Within the Covert Action intelligence operations one may find drug and terrorist activities. There seems to be strong debate on whether terrorists are state sponsored or not state sponsored, because it depends on the perpetrators of the hostile activities. In sophisticated operations prior to 1984 there were perps who were state sponsored and the activities generally preceded actual fighting and hostilities such as war.

Eventually, Mr. Peake hired me as a secretary. Before I qualified for the position that got me out of the mail room, I had to study and prepare for the agency's typist test. I passed it, typing 64 words a minute. Our deeper and more important relationship started on the day I reported to his office and began working as a secretary in 1961. I was another step closer to my dream.

The job was challenging because I had to type error-free CIA correspondence for the FBI. Erasures were discouraged. Most of the letters I typed were addressed to the FBI, and were signed by Mr. Peake or other senior Agency officials. As I said, Mr. Peake led the Counter Intelligence Section of the Branch. It was logical and necessary for that section to prepare correspondence between the Agency and the FBI. Information about US citizens and activities from abroad had to be passed to the Bureau. So, as the secretary, naturally I typed the correspondence. The information was classified because it came from CIA sources. That is the real sensitivity in Agency work. It isn't that the details of individual's interactions are secret, but the source always remains classified. The source **must** be protected.

Also during this period, in my free time, I pushed forward toward my college degree. I majored in chemistry with a minor in mathematics at the former Washington, D.C., Teachers College, now part of the University of the District of Columbia. Mr. Peake did me a great favor by granting me permission to work on my studies during working hours, as long as I had completed my work for the day. This was just one of many great favors from Mr. Peake that led to my advancement.

While I was working as a secretary for Mr. Peake, the opportunity to work abroad came up. The Chief of Station (OS) at the Far Northern Country (FNC) and one of the European Chief's began discussing a position in a mail-room in the FNC that I could do. (Note that this FNC has no name in that it would be contrary to the confidentiality of the work and thus not publishable at this time.) On with the story and as fate would have it the COS was Big Post and the Chief's secretary was Helen Zirnite, one of the other two Roosevelt High School classmates that were hired with me. Mr. Big Post, began a dialogue about me to determine if I could handle the new position. Helen Zirnite in addition to sharing the good news with me was able to include her superior and the negotiations went very well. The Chief discussed and decided whether I was right for the mail room position in the FNC. They had agreed that they wanted a male to work the mail room because of the weight of the pouches.

I also had two godfathers, Mr. Rogers and Mr. Peake, who negotiated and ensured that I obtained our first highly desirable assignment abroad. Eventually, I was contacted and invited to accept a position overseas in the FNC. Happily, my wife, Rose and our three children (De Levay, Monique and Leutrell II) came on our first residential assignment abroad in 1963. Leutrell II was born December 16, 1960 in Washington, D.C. the same year that my mother died.

The dream was pulling me forward across the ocean. It was our first of many foreign countries. Little did I imagine I would meet another Dreamer there. I have said there are 15 Intelligence Community agencies and departments because that was the count as of 04/25/05 when I first

started writing my story. However, prior to 1984 there were thirteen. The NGA and Homeland Security Department had not been organized. By the time you read this there may be more, or less.

Chapter 3:

Assignment to a Far Northern European Country (FNC)

In October 1963, I was assigned abroad to work as CIA mail clerk in the FNC.

Our family settled into the country and began to transition easily into our new lifestyle. Our stay began at a hotel in a downtown area. My wife, Rose, and our three children -- De Levay, age 5; Monique, age 4, and Leutrell II, age 3 -- managed to stay busy. They met people at the hotel and spent leisure time in the shopping area between the hotel and normal tourist attractions downtown.

Our third child, Leutrell Michael Carlton Osborne II, born on December 16, 1960, was now with us. Unfortunately, my mother Ella did not get to see Leutrell II, since she passed just before he came into the world. Because he was so young, Leutrell II suffered most in learning English while living in a foreign country. He overcame his language learning confusion, but it was a challenge for us all at the time.

My cover organization leased a fantastic house for us in the suburbs. Having the house leased by the cover organization was one of the perks of being overseas. The four bedrooms were on the first landing and the living room and kitchen were on the second level. The study was positioned on the level between the first and second floors. It was an upside down split-level.

Because I developed another godfather, Robert Harvard at the FNC Station, I also had opportunities to begin learning the craft of intelligence, as former DCI Allen Dulles called it. I mentioned Dulles as the first Agency DCI whom I observed during my early days with the Agency. My outside activities in the FNC enabled me to use my street skills in meeting people and winning friends. I gradually acquired Agency skills in assessing foreigners for their potential value in performing intelligence work. Though I was not yet a Case Officer, I was still keeping my dream very much alive. I continued learning the craft of intelligence and I did do some activities that definitely prepared me for the next phase of my life in CIA. I gathered information and uncovered secrets regarding the activities of various foreign nations in the FNC. Mr. Harvard guided me in writing and filing my reports. Some of my reporting contributed to valuable support of my government's national and international security operations.

All was well, except that when we first arrived in our new home, President John F. Kennedy was assassinated and we didn't know anything about it for the entire weekend. Naturally, we were stunned like the rest of the world. Like most people, I vividly remember that instant I found out. While I was walking to catch the train to the city, one of the neighbors picked me up and gave me a lift to the city where I worked. This was the Monday morning after the assassination. The neighbor asked me if I had heard that "They killed the murderer of the President." Even today, I still hear his words.

I was caught completely off guard and thought that my neighbor was having a struggle speaking English. I needed further explanation and he obliged. I was in a state of shock when I walked into the office. I was numb. I could not call Rose because our telephone had not been turned on. She had to wait until I got home to hear the horrendous news. We had been out of it because we weren't watching television because it had not been converted to European standards. We did not have our household goods, so we did not have a radio. Further, we did not know the language. We had been out to the stores that Saturday but had not noticed the headlines.

Though this event formed the background of our relocation, we quickly began assimilating into the community. We made use of all of the local facilities. The kids went to the outdoor children's facility, where there was plenty of playground equipment and fresh air. We did not have any health problems, especially among the children. It seemed they improved their health just by being there and playing outdoors every day.

We made friends in the neighborhood and soon were invited to social events. We had several baby-sitters, which allowed Rose and I to participate in a number of social activities arranged by my cover organization. We enjoyed meeting new friends and speaking their native language with them. The children also learned the language quickly and made many new friends among their peers.

I was able to continue my college education at the local university and was also deeply involved with social activities of the university's Foreign Students Club. Of course, many of my social encounters enabled me to blend into the society, and position myself so that I could eventually successfully conduct my business as an aspiring CIA Case Officer. My chief objectives were to make contact with my real targets, residing and traveling abroad. During the two and half years in the FNC, I did meet a few and even hosted some in our home.

Before we moved into our home, we knew the landlord planned eventually to sell the property. So when we received the notice to vacate about six months later, we were prepared and moved across town into another fantastic house. It was a giant log cabin with two stories and two separate wings. The children used the downstairs space of one wing as a playroom. We used a nearby room for entertaining. Our living room, which was equipped with a fireplace, was just outstanding. We had many parties and continued the good life, socializing, learning the language and acclimating to the culture.

I discovered that Horacio Jones, another Black from my high school in Washington, DC, had secured an assignment to the U.S. Embassy in Oslo, Norway. This was a wonderful break for us. We traveled back and forth to between cities and met regularly. We discussed a variety of important matters, including the intricacies of living abroad. We were particularly interested in the lifestyles of unaccompanied American females, especially Mina and Pat, who were clerics like us. These young ladies happened to be assigned in Oslo. Both eventually married Norwegians. Mina introduced Rose and me to one of the few Black females residing in Oslo, Betty Roach of New Jersey.

Horacio and I discussed the Oslo University Student Union meetings. We were both intrigued by the Blacks from back home who would show up to talk with them based on the outreach efforts of the Embassy. We talked about the appearance of John Lewis in Oslo on behalf of the United States Information Agency (USIA). Mr. Lewis was removed from his position as leader of Student Nonviolent Coordinating Committee (SNCC) on the very day he was speaking to the members of the student union. Lewis went on to become a Congressman (D-Georgia).

Horacio and I also discussed the events surrounding the visit to Oslo by Dr. C. Eric Lincoln, Duke University professor of religion. Dr. Lincoln also came on behalf of USIA to speak to the Norwegian students. Dr. Lincoln had written a groundbreaking book on the Black Muslims (Nation of Islam).

Horacio made it his business to make contact with certain visitors to Oslo. He buttonholed Dr. Lincoln and that's how I got to meet Dr. Lincoln. Dr. Lincoln later became more important to me, after we had developed a friendship. As a very bright and encouraging spirit, he ultimately recommended the title for my story: <u>Black Man in the CIA</u>.

While I was in the FNC and Horacio was in Oslo, there was a Black Ambassador to Norway named Clifton Wharton as well as a Black Ambassador to Finland named Carl Rowan. Horacio and I talked extensively about these two gentlemen. They were like night and day according to Horacio, who had firsthand knowledge of Wharton, because they worked together at the embassy in Oslo. We compared notes on the two ambassadors. Horacio said he always waited for Ambassador Wharton to uphold Black people in public when news articles were published in Norwegian newspapers about the U.S. Civil Rights Movement. Wharton remained the model professional diplomat, never proclaiming any public support for a particular group, not even his own cultural group. Ambassador Rowan was far different. The newspapers carried headlines on his actions and statements, and quoted him regularly whenever he eloquently talked about civil rights issues. About this time, Horacio was ready to achieve his greatest feat ever when he acquired seats for the Noble Peace Prize Ceremony and for the US Ambassador's Reception for Rose and myself.

Chapter 4:

Meeting Dr. Martin Luther King, Jr.

Just imagine my excitement when Rose and I had an opportunity to attend the Nobel Peace Prize honoring Dr. Martin Luther King, Jr., in Oslo, Norway on Friday, December 10, 1964. Horacio Jones, a friend from Washington, DC had secured a position with the Department of State at the U.S. Embassy in Oslo, Norway. Horacio got the word early and engineered our attendance at both the Noble Peace Prize ceremony and the official, invitation-only reception given by Ambassador Madame Joy Tibbits in honor of Dr. King. I never knew how Horacio achieved both feats. Obviously, he used his Embassy connections. The copies of the tickets, invitation and guest list follow:

honor of Dr. Martin Luther

The Ambassador of the United States of America

requests the honor of the company of

Mr. and Mrs. Osborne

at a reception

on Friday, December eleven

at 2045 - 2130 o'clock

R.S.V.P.

belegate 28

X- 803

Adgangskort

til

utdelingen av Nobels Fredspris 1964

i Universitetets Aula

Torsdag den 10de desember 1964 kl. 13.

Ståplass

Formiddagsantrekk

In Honor of Dr. Martin Luther King, Jr.

List of Dr. Martin Luther King Jr. Party:

Dr. and Mrs. Martin Luther King, Jr.
Dr. and Mrs. Ralph D. Abernathy
Rev. Richard Battles
Mrs. Septima Clark
Mrs. Dorothy Cotton
Mrs. Christine Farris
Miss Carole Hoover
Mrs. Lillie Hunter
Rev. Logan Kearse
Rev. A. D. King
Dr. and Mrs. Martin Luther King, Sr.
Rev. Bernard Lee
Mrs. Marion Logan
Mr. Louis Martin
Mr. Noel Marder
Miss Rita McClain
Miss Dora McDonald
Mrs. Nina Miller
Dr. Lawrence Reddick
Rev. Milton Reid
Mr. Bayard Rustin
Mr. and Mrs. Harry Wachtel
Mr. Wyatt Walker
Rev. Andrew Young
Atty. Chauncey Eskridge
Dr. Charles Ireland
Mr. Monita Sleet
Mr. Charles Sanders
Rev. D. M. Hoover
Mr. Robert Mitchell
Rev. Richard Dixon
Mrs. Freddye Henderson
Bishop and Mrs. Smallwood Williams
Mr. William L. Rowe
Rev. Gordon

OTHER GUESTS:

H.E. the Prime Minister and Mrs. Einar Gerhardsen
H.E. the Minister of Foreign Affairs and Mrs. Halvard Lange
H.E. the Minister of Defense, Dr. Gudmund Harlem
H.E. the Minister of Church and Education and Mrs. Helge Sivertsen
H.E. the Minister of Finance and Mrs. Andreas Cappelen
H.E. the Minister of Justice and Police and Mrs. Oscar C. Gundersen
H.E. the Minister of Municipal and Labor Affairs and Mrs. Jens Haugland
H.E. the Minister of Social Affairs and Mrs. Olav Gjaerevoll
H.E. the Minister of Commerce and Shipping, Trygve Lie
H.E. the Minister of Fisheries and Mrs. Magnus Andersen
H.E. the Minister of Industry and Mrs. Karl Trasti
H.E. the Minister of Agriculture and Mrs. Leif Granli

(cont.)

53

(cont.):

H.E. the Minister of Communications and Mrs. Eric Himle
H.E. the Minister of Family and Consumer Affairs and Mr. Kurt Jonas Bjørkholt
H.E. the Minister of Prices and Wages and Mrs. Idar Norstrand
H.E. the President of the Storting and Mrs. Nils Langhelle
H.E. the Vice President of the Storting and Mrs. Alv Kjøs
H.E. the President of the Lagting and Mrs. Nils Hønsvald
H.E. the President of the Odelsting and Mrs. Per Borten
H.E. the Vice President of the Lagting and Mrs. Einar Hareide
H.E. the Vice President of the Odelsting and Mrs. Jakob Pettersen
H.E. the Secretary General and Mrs. Johan C. A. Raeder
H.E. the Under Secretary and Mrs. Jens M. Boyesen
H.E. the Under Secretary Dagfin Juel
H.E. the Mayor of Oslo and Mrs. Brynjulf Bull
Mr. and Mrs. Jens Evensen
Mr. and Mrs. Einar Ansteensen
Mr. and Mrs. Jahn N. Halvorsen
H.E. the Chief of Protocol and Mrs. Ditlef Knudsen
Mr. and Mrs. Tor Myklebost
Mr. and Mrs. Andreas Andersen
H.E. the Chief Justice and Mrs. Terje Wold
Mr. and Mrs. Terje Baalsrud
Mr. and Mrs. Erling Bergendahl
Mr. and Mrs. Rolf D. Bibow
Mr. and Mrs. Derek Blix
Mr. and Mrs. Hans Borgen
Mr. and Mrs. Trygve Bratteli
Mr. and Mrs. Christian A. S. Christensen
Mr. and Mrs. John M. Donovan
Mr. and Mrs. Torolf Elster
Mr. Harold Galloway
Mr. and Mrs. Gunnar Garbo
Dr. and Mrs. Tore Gjelsvik
Mr. and Mrs. Johan Hambro
Mr. and Mrs. Reidar Hirsti
Mr. and Mrs. Bjarne Høye
Mr. Gunnar Jahn
Mr. and Mrs. Torolv Kandahl
Mr. and Mrs. Birger Kildal
Reverend and Mrs. Myrus Knutson
Mr. and Mrs. Haakon Lie
Mr. and Mrs. Sjur Lindebraekke
Mr. and Mrs. Kurt Jonas Lionaess
Mr. and Mrs. Karl Lyche
Mr. and Mrs. John Daniel Lyng
Mr. and Mrs. Finn Moe
Mr. and Mrs. Otto Naes
Mr. and Mrs. Hans Fridtjof Nielsen
Mr. and Mrs. Konrad M. Nordahl
Dr. and Mrs. Nils Ørvik
Mr. and Mrs. Gunnar Natvig Pedersen

(cont.)

54

Reverend and Mrs. H. Paxton
Mr. and Mrs. Bent Røiseland
Mr. and Mrs. Rognerud (Mrs. Berte)
Mr. and Mrs. August Schou
Dr. and Mrs. John Sannes
Mr. and Mrs. Rolf Semmingsen
Mr. and Mrs. Hans Kr. Schou
Mr. and Mrs. Gustav Søderland
Mr. and Mrs. Per Strand
Mr. and Mrs. Axel Strøm
Mrs. Willy Sveen
Mr. and Mrs. Arvid Sveum
Mr. and Mrs. Sverre Syversen
Mr. and Mrs. Jens Aage Tellefsen
Mr. and Mrs. Hans Jakob Ustvedt
Rektor and Mrs. Hans Vogt
Mr. and Mrs. Ragnar Vold
Mr. and Mrs. Erling Wickborg
Mr. and Mrs. George Anderson
Miss Beko
Mr. and Mrs. Carolan
Mr. and Mrs. Elliott
Mr. and Mrs. Flaata
Miss Ford
Mr. and Mrs. Goplen
Col. and Mrs. Goff
Mr. and Mrs. Griggs
Mr. and Mrs. Holm
Mr. and Mrs. Irons
Miss Jackson
Mr. and Mrs. Jorgensen
Col. and Mrs. Johnsen
Mr. Laase
Mr. Mansfield
Miss Massey
Mr. and Mrs. Mellor
Mr. and Mrs. Morley
Mr. and Mrs. O'Grady
Mr. and Mrs. Olsson
Mr. and Mrs. Leutrell Osborne
Captain and Mrs. Olson
Mr. and Mrs. Porter
Mr. and Mrs. Schilling
Mr. and Mrs. Sena
Mr. and Mrs. Schute
Mr. and Mrs. Tolf
Miss Weyres

We were there at the Nobel Peace Prize ceremony in Oslo, Norway that was held at the Great Hall at 1:15 pm. on Thursday, December 10, 1964. In short we witnessed history being made with Dr. Martin Luther King, Jr. receiving the Nobel Peace Prize. It was unimaginable that Rose and I would be there when Dr. King, the social change pioneer, was awarded this great honor. The historic ceremony convened in magnificent style in the Great Hall. It looked much like an old church down south, back in the USA, with a broad balcony and row upon row of pews about 50 deep. We were fortunate to obtain seats in the balcony, which gave us an excellent view for taking in the entire affair. The event still stands as one of the most memorable experiences of my life.

We sat next to the wife of Bishop Smallwood Williams, a famous preacher from Washington, D.C., who started his church by preaching outdoors. He would stand on a D.C. sidewalk at an intersection; dozens of people at a time, sitting in their cars, became a captive audience for his stirring oratory.

As I looked around, taking in the electricity of the moment, I found it amazing that simply by coincidence, I was witnessing American history take place miles away from her shores while sitting with three Black people from her capital city attending the Nobel Peace Prize in Oslo, Norway. We were not the only Blacks at the affair besides Dr. King's people and possibly a few other visitors. We found it very interesting that some whites in attendance said they had never seen so many Black people in their lives. In the late 60s there were no more than ten African American families living in Oslo. No more than twenty students from Africa were enrolled at the University of Oslo.

December 10, 1964
Oslo, Norway

I accept the Nobel Prize for Peace at a moment when twenty-two million Negroes of the United States of America are engaged in a creative battle to end the long night of racial injustice. I accept this award on behalf of a civil rights movement which is moving with determination and a majestic scorn for risk and danger to establish a reign of freedom and a rule of justice.

I am mindful that only yesterday in Birmingham, Alabama, our children, crying out for brotherhood, were answered with fire hoses, snarling dogs and even death. I am mindful that only yesterday in Philadelphia, Mississippi, young people seeking to secure the right to vote were brutalized and murdered. And only yesterday more than 40 houses of worship in the State of Mississippi alone were bombed or burned because they offered a sanctuary to those who would not accept segregation.

I am mindful that debilitating and grinding poverty afflicts my people and chains them to the lowest rung of the economic ladder.

Therefore, I must ask why this prize is awarded to a movement which is beleaguered and committed to unrelenting struggle; to a movement which has not won the very peace and brotherhood which is the essence of the Nobel Prize.

After contemplation, I conclude that this award which I receive on behalf of that movement is profound recognition that nonviolence is the answer to the crucial political and moral question of our time -- the need for man to overcome oppression and violence without resorting to violence and oppression.

Civilization and violence are antithetical concepts. Negroes of the United States, following the people of India, have demonstrated that nonviolence is not sterile passivity, but a powerful moral force which makes for social transformation. Sooner or later all the people of the world will have to discover a way to live together in peace, and thereby transform this pending cosmic elegy into a creative psalm of brotherhood.

If this is to be achieved, man must evolve for all human conflict a method which rejects revenge, aggression and retaliation. The foundation of such a method is love. The tortuous road which has led from Montgomery, Alabama, to Oslo bears witness to this truth. This is a road over which millions of Negroes are traveling to find a new sense of dignity.

This same road has opened for all Americans a new era of progress and hope. It has led to a new Civil Rights bill, and it will, I am convinced, be widened and lengthened into a superhighway of justice as Negro and white men in increasing numbers create alliances to overcome their common problems.

I accept this award today with an abiding faith in America and an audacious faith in the future of mankind. I refuse to accept despair as the final response to the ambiguities of history. I refuse to accept the idea that the "isness" of man's present nature makes him morally incapable of reaching up for the eternal "oughtness" that forever confronts him.

I refuse to accept the idea that man is mere flotsam and jetsam in the river of life unable to influence the unfolding events which surround him. I refuse to accept the view that mankind is so tragically bound to the starless midnight of racism and war that the bright daybreak of peace and brotherhood can never become a reality.

I refuse to accept the cynical notion that nation after nation must spiral down a militaristic stairway into the hell of thermonuclear destruction. I believe that unarmed truth and unconditional love will have the final word in reality. This is why right temporarily defeated is stronger than evil triumphant.

I believe that even amid today's motor bursts and whining bullets, there is still hope for a brighter tomorrow. I believe that wounded justice, lying prostrate on the blood-flowing streets of our nations, can be lifted from this dust of shame to reign supreme among the children of men.

I have the audacity to believe that peoples everywhere can have three meals a day for their bodies, education and culture for their minds, and dignity, equality and freedom for their spirits. I believe that what self-centered men have torn down, men other-centered can build up. I still believe that one day mankind will bow before the altars of God and be crowned triumphant over war and bloodshed, and nonviolent redemptive goodwill will proclaim the rule of the land.

"And the lion and the lamb shall lie down together and every man shall sit under his own vine and fig tree and none shall be afraid."

I still believe that we shall overcome.

This faith can give us courage to face the uncertainties of the future. It will give our tired feet new strength as we continue our forward stride toward the city of freedom. When our days become dreary with low-hovering clouds and our nights become darker than a thousand midnights, we will know that we are living in the creative turmoil of a genuine civilization struggling to be born.

Today I come to Oslo as a trustee, inspired and with renewed dedication to humanity. I accept this prize on behalf of all men who love peace and brotherhood. I say I come as a trustee, for in the depths of my heart I am aware that this prize is much more than an honor to me personally.

Every time I take a flight I am always mindful of the many people who make a successful journey possible -- the known pilots and the unknown ground crew.

So you honor the dedicated pilots of our struggle who have sat at the controls as the freedom movement soared into orbit. You honor, once again, Chief (Albert) Luthuli of South Africa, whose struggles with and for his people, who are still met with the most brutal expression of man's inhumanity to man.

You honor the ground crew without whose labor and sacrifices the jet flights to freedom could never have left the earth.

Most of these people will never make the headlines and their names will not appear in *Who's Who*. Yet when years have rolled past and when the blazing light of truth is focused on this marvelous age in which we live -- men and women will know and children will be taught that we have a finer land, a better people, a more noble civilization -- because these humble children of God were willing to suffer for righteousness' sake.

I think Alfred Nobel would know what I mean when I say that I accept this award in the spirit of a curator of some precious heirloom which he holds in trust for its true owners -- all those to whom beauty is truth and truth beauty -- and in whose eyes the beauty of genuine brotherhood and peace is more precious than diamonds or silver or gold.

MARTIN LUTHER KING, JR

http://www.nobelprizes.com/nobel/peace/MLK-nobel.html

Chapter 5:

The Black Agenda - Dr. Martin Luther King, Jr.

Being overseas assigned to the FNC meant that I had to live thousands of miles away from the USA during some of her most tumultuous days. It meant that I could not join in and experience first hand some of the major achievements of the Civil Rights Movement. As a matter of fact, I missed the March on Washington in 1963 because I was receiving training for the assignment in the FNC. To suddenly find myself at the right place and right time to be thrust into the midst of all the international buzz and excitement being poured upon the central figure of America's social upheaval was pure magic and serendipity.

The next evening proved as or more exciting. On Friday, December 11, 1964, at the residence of the U.S. Ambassador, Madame Joy Tibbits,.Rose and I met Dr. King and his wife, Coretta King again. The Ambassador's reception for Dr. King, was scheduled from 8:45 pm. through 10:30 pm., giving me the chance to have a one-on-one, corner-of-the-room chat with Dr. King. On looking back at our meeting at the Ambassador's residence, I called our talk "the Black Agenda." At the time, I felt great pride just being in his presence and standing eye-to-eye with him. The only way to describe the experience was that it was awe-inspiring. As fate would have it, I was one of the first to hear his reflections on his life after being awarded The Nobel Peace Prize.

While it was thrilling to meet Dr. King and his wife, Coretta, the experience was not without disappointments. Most diplomats and their spouses left early in my opinion, ruining the reception and denying Dr. King, Jr. precious moments to bask in the social spotlight and hob knob with guests. It was as if the white diplomats from around the world were saying in unison, "Yes, we honor you as a world hero, but we are not giving you equal treatment."

They treated this auspicious event as if it were some normal everyday diplomatic affair where the people come, "show the flag" and leave. Yes, it is like some people do when they go to a wake and leave right after the viewing. It was a sad picture. Dr. King and his wife actually looked lonely in that vast room -- stars of a party that never happened. Dr. King was calm, cool, and collected. He looked as if nothing happened. So be it, Rose and I thought. The early departure of the diplomats enabled us to talk extensively with Dr. and Mrs. King.

I paired off with him and Rose with Coretta. We pursued our separate discussions for about a solid hour without interruption in a corner of the huge and almost empty reception hall. For me, Dr. King had the calming effect of a person who loved himself so he could reach out and love others. It is special to connect with such an exceptional individual, because so few are available. Perhaps His Spirit was in charge of ego much more than one can imagine.

My conversation with Dr. King focused on the Civil Rights Movement, which was still progressing back home. We spoke in terms of the "Black Agenda." Overseas serving my country, I was starved for any news of events back home, especially news affecting Blacks. Now I stood toe-to-toe, and eye-to-eye listening to this insider of all insiders of the Black Agenda telling me the news firsthand. We talked about the Southern Christian Leadership Conference (SCLC) and especially the August 28, 1963, March on Washington. Dr. King said that the event, from his vantage point, was a day of high celebration for the leaders and supporters of the civil rights movement.

He told me about the April 1963 Birmingham march and described how he had been jailed. He commented about the famous "Letter from Birmingham Jail" that he wrote in response to white clergymen who had issued a statement calling him and his movement's activities unwise and untimely.

Dr. King told me about his belief in "non-violence direct action," a freedom fighting strategy initiated in the early 1900's during the Indian struggle for equality in Apartheid South Africa by Mahatma Gandhi, the humble, yet powerful, Indian leader. Dr. King said the non-violence direct action strategy is intended to create tension so that an oppressive power that has constantly refused to negotiate with the oppressed is forced to confront change.

Dr. King counted on white moderates in the USA to function as allies and to embrace non-violence and vigorously support the Black struggle for freedom. However, he said, he was disappointed with the white moderates because they talked a good game, but they attempted only weakly to be catalysts for change.

Dr. King told me about the Congress of Racial Equality (CORE) and the Student Nonviolent Coordinating Committee (SNCC). CORE pushed for the end of segregation, especially in public transportation down south, while the SNCC led national voter registration campaigns. Members of CORE and SNCC participated in the Freedom Rides. He explained that there were battles among the leaders of the two Civil Rights groups. Each side wanted dominance. They fought for turf and were sometimes both alternately bitter and friendly. Much of their activities focused on fund raising, for money is power.

Dr. King mentioned H. Rap Brown and linked him with Ralph Featherstone. This was very interesting to me because Ralph and I had attended the same high school and college. Dr. King said both of them were involved in the SNCC. Dr. King was surprised that I personally knew Featherstone. I told Dr. King that we went to Roosevelt High School and D.C. Teacher's College together. Ralph, along with others, such as Curtis Taylor, another high school classmate, were the athletic types or "jocks" at Roosevelt. I was a cadet, Junior ROTC, type. However, I knew that Ralph was very smart, like the other African Americans at my school, who were in the "grand experiment," attending Roosevelt during the late 1950s.

In order to get into the desegregated high school back in 1956 an African American student had to have a high IQ. The barriers changed as the years went on and fewer non-African Americans attended Roosevelt. I told Dr. King that Ralph was a speech major at D.C. Teachers College. Featherstone really had to buckle down and work hard to achieve. Even with high IQ's, most African Americans had to really apply themselves to achieve good grades and respect at D.C. Teachers.

We also discussed Congressman Walter Fauntroy's activities in Washington, D.C. My connection was that Walter's brother, Raymond; he and I had been in the Boy Scouts together at the YMCA in D.C.

Dr. King asked me: "What religion do you practice? I told him: "I am a Roman Catholic." He found that interesting because he understood that there were three Popes of African descent and that significant events in the Roman Catholic Church occurred during their reigns. He said, "I only remember a few details about the one Pope named Melchiades I and that he had signed the Edict of Milan. He said, "Another African Pope was responsible for organizing the Church Sacraments." Neither Dr. King nor I had enough details. I later found that not only were there three African Popes, all three are also Saints. They are Victor (189-203 AD), Gelasius (492-496 AD), and Melchiades or Miltiades (311-314 AD).

Later in the conversation I asked Dr. King about the Black Muslims, also known as the Nation of Islam (NOI). The activities of Black leaders and organizations were naturally of more interest to me and other African Americans living abroad than to the foreign nationals among whom we lived. It seemed as if we were starved for information on civil rights and news from back home about our African American communities.

I did not have any information on the Black Muslims, except for Dr. C. Eric Lincoln's book on the Nation of Islam. Dr. King said that the NOI had many problems with the civil authorities. However, the Muslims, according to him, had success in rehabilitating African Americans who came out of the penal system. Dr. King felt that the success of the Muslims was in part attributable to the fact that the convicts received a sense of purpose and religion – a moral compass.

Horacio told me that in Oslo, there was basically a white out on information about Black America. News about African Americans was not of interest to the Norwegians; African Americans rarely visited them. It was not a simple thing for either one of us to learn about "Black events in America." So, I found myself eagerly listening to Dr. King as he gave me the latest news and developments about my brothers and sisters back home.

Dr. King said that Elijah Muhammad, who believed that the solution to the race problem was in separating the races, had established himself as a strong leader of the NOI. Dr. King believed that the NOI resented white civil authorities. I asked Dr. King about Malcolm X and his exit from the NOI. He said that Malcolm X was organizing the Muslim Mosque, Inc. in New York City. Malcolm still believed Elijah Muhammad was a follower of the NOI, and indicated that the Muslim Mosque was not to rival the NOI. According to Dr. King at this time he believed that Malcolm X still held to the separation of the races but taught retaliation only in self-defense.

It was refreshing to hear about how African Americans were evolving politically and socially. Our conversation ended with very favorable pleasantries as he and I left the reception with our wives.

At that time, I did not realize how important my chance meeting with Dr. King would be because I had placed him only in the context of his being honored with the Nobel Peace Prize. Conversely, he had not been aware of the fact that he had been opening up a treasure trove of personal insights to a CIA employee.

The world now knows that his fame grew after Oslo. As for me, I had come to a crossroads. All the fortunate events that had led to my momentous meeting with this world-class Dreamer had shown me that "the journey is the destination." All the events of my life had conspired so I could share these magic moments with a man whose own bigger dream echoed in my awareness. Though Dr. King didn't deliver his "I've been to the mountaintop" speech until 1968, I felt as if I had personally been to one with this great mentor in his own moment of tremendous honor and global acknowledgment.

Ironically, Dr. King told me that many of his followers and supporters suspected that the government was watching him and other leading figures of the movement. He didn't have all the details, he said. However, he strongly suspected that he and his lieutenants were being monitored.

"They're watching me.", said Dr. King. "The government is watching my organization and me."

Though, I always clearly remembered his comments, it was only later that I was able to make the connections to King's surveillance and "dirty tricks" by the FBI. In this case, I had personal knowledge that the Agency had not been tasked by the FBI with any requirements to monitor him nor his people while they were in Oslo, Norway. The conversation with Dr. King was a milestone that gave me the opportunity to see that his mission on planet earth was identical to mine. That is, we share the mission of justice, peace and fair play as does every human being on earth whether we are aware of and embrace it or not.

Dr. King knew me as a passionate 25-year-old Black youngster -- if I may say it, a D.C. Negro with a clerical position abroad. At that time in history, few Blacks were given opportunities to perform sophisticated roles in the United States government intelligence activities. So I am sure he felt comfortable expressing his true feelings given he was a 35-year-old Black man who had already been through considerable trials and tribulations as a Civil Rights leader being honored with the Nobel Peace Prize. I doubt that he saw me as a threat, given that I was still a rookie in the game of life.

But another leg of the journey lay ahead as my own dream continued to unfold. My journey as a Black Man in the CIA was just beginning. Working behind the scenes in various other countries; I began to leave my mark as an intelligence professional. Often life serves up triumph and tragedy in the same meal. On the personal side of things, a tragic event was about to leave its mark on my family and myself

A Personal Tragedy

Though our meeting Dr. King indeed was a peak experience, unfortunately into each life comes some sadness. After enjoying great happiness, we were about to plunge into the crucible of grief.

Rose and I had a daughter born in the FNC in May 1965. Her name was Rose Anastasia Osborne. She was a joy to us all. The older children enjoyed baby Rose, and we were a happy family until suddenly one morning, De Levay and Leutrell found Rose Anastasia dead in her crib. The older children woke us, and we rushed to the crib, and then just stood there looking at the baby's corpse and feeling totally devastated. Being in a foreign country, we had no extended family to help us bear this emotional burden.

There is nothing normal about losing a child. After the initial shock, Rose and I reacted quite differently. Rose was numb and had a great deal of trouble accepting the fact that Rose Anastasia was dead. She just could not believe it had happened. She repeatedly questioned, "What happened? … How did it happen? … Who was at fault? And could it have been prevented? What could we have done differently to prevent this?" Of course, we did not have any answers for the strange crib death. I requested an autopsy and made funeral arrangements. We sent for Rose's mother, Inez Powell Dade, and prepared for the funeral. Even though I had buried many relatives before, including my mother, Ella, my uncle Henry Vander Lippe, my grandfather William Grisby, those experiences did not prepare me for making arrangements for my own eleven month-old baby girl.

My mother-in-law, Inez Powell Dade, arrived. She had never traveled outside of the United States before, and here she was leaving home to attend her granddaughter's funeral thousands of miles away. What a sad yet momentous event it was for her. Grandmother's presence helped relieve some of the stress because only she could help Rose cope.

The outpouring of sympathy and condolences from people near and far was immeasurable. US Embassy personnel, U.S. and foreign diplomats and non-diplomats alike, expressed their sympathy. The local Catholic parish near our home was filled to capacity for the funeral ceremony. It was as if it were Sunday morning. Ultimately, our family re-grouped but it took a long time before we gained full acceptance of what happened to our daughter. The loving daughter whose life was cut short; only being with us for less than a year. In that year she had brought such warmth and happiness into our world that she would never be forgotten.

The autopsy revealed that Rose Anastasia had an inoperable heart condition and a malformed artery. There was nothing anyone could have done to prevent the tragedy, even if we had discovered the condition earlier. We shipped Anastasia home to Washington for burial. Rose's eldest sister Helen handled the affairs for us.

Though this tragic event stalled us for a short period, we were young and full of vitality, so we snapped back, completed our tour in the FNC and at the appropriate time returned to Washington D. C. Unfortunately, the Agency did not assign me to a position before I left the FNC, so I knew I would have to work hard to win a meaningful position that could help me continue to develop as a case officer. I began pumping myself up so much that I began to dream of making the major shift from a non-professional to a professional position. I began to envision with great clarity that I could and would become a spy master.

We were returning to Washington in 1966 from the Far Northern European Country. Headquarters had not assigned me a definite job so I took matters into my own hands. Rose and I discussed my networking plan to get a job and complete my education. Although while in the FNC, I had continued college by taking more science and mathematics, I still was short almost two years of the degree I wanted.

I knew I wanted to get into the Agency's professional training program, the CTP, but I did not know how to do that. By 1966, I had acquired a healthy number of undergraduate course credits. My desire to complete college grew because I realized that a Case Officer with a college education functioned better than one without. At the same time, I still suffered from "stinking thinking." Before I joined the Agency, lack of money had dampened my natural enthusiasm for improving our lot. In short, early on I did not aspire to get a college degree because I had an experience that I let kill my desire. I let family circumstances of "not having the money" overshadow my dreams and aspirations. I felt a stirring deep inside that told me I had the potential, should the opportunity arise. That part of me never gave up.

On entering the Agency, I knew that I needed a college education in order to achieve my objective of becoming a Case Officer but denied it until a few months after I was on duty. Also, by 1966 I knew about Justice Arrow who was the first Black Case Officer to desegregate the Case Officer ranks. This exceptional event happened under the watch of former DCI Richard Helms, who was then head of the Directorate of Operations. Even Justice Arrow himself was not able to tell me how and why it happened. However, it did happen in 1957.

Since I had to be sure about my next Headquarters assignment, I used my network of contacts in 1966. As a matter of fact, I took some of my home leave time to make contact with Mr. Rogers and Ms. High Heels. I knew Mr. Rogers and Ms. High Heels before we went overseas. We all worked in the same Branch of the European Division.

I had great respect for Mr. Rogers and already considered him one of my godfathers. He was instrumental in assisting me to obtain the assignment in the FNC. When I contacted him in 1966, he still was in my corner and agreed to arrange for me to have the personnel department assess my potential as a Case Officer. In short, that meant he arranged for me to be tested for aptitude to become a Career Trainee in the CIA's Career Training Program (CTP). The results were not conclusive at the time, but I did get enough encouragement to know I could make it as an Agency Case Officer. I held onto that insight to drive my desire to get into the CTP. This dream would not let me go.

Chapter 6:

Earned PHD in Intelligence Before My Bachelors

I earned my PhD in the Espionage Enterprise (EE) before I got my undergraduate degree. That is, I completed the CIA Career Training Program (CTP) in 1969 before I obtained my undergraduate degree from The American University, Washington, DC in 1971 -- my Bachelor of Science degree in Political Science.

My "dream-mojo" was still with me and perhaps a guardian angel or two. The Career Training Program (CTP) is the Agency training program that resulted in my "PhD in Intelligence." The graduates of the CTP enter the training from both the inside and outside of the Agency. To get the all around experience needed for their continued success they get to lead and operate the Agency in all four Directorates. The CTP graduates are spread throughout the Agency in various positions. I will describe the events that led to my virtual graduate degree in Intelligence as well as some other educational experiences before completing my undergraduate degree.

Note, I don't use the term "intelligence" since what I really know is the "Espionage Enterprise" (EE). In my world at the CIA, "intelligence" was a term that refers to the information products that are analyzed and turned into finished intelligence products. These documents originate in the Directorate of Intelligence (DI) and are disseminated to the national Intelligence Community, especially the White House. So, I prefer to use the EE or 'Espionage Enterprise' terminology.

The opportunity to get into CTP came in 1968, almost three years after I had established myself in the Western Hemisphere Division with the assistance of Ms. High Heels. Earlier in my life I had not planned to go to college because we did not have the money but by 1958 I realized I would not move up in the Agency without that valuable college degree. Undaunted, I decided to attend D.C. Teachers College. I went there a total of 12 years, majoring in chemistry and with a minor in mathematics. As I said, I took courses even while I was overseas. Between 1966 - 1968, I returned to D.C. Teachers College for evening classes.

It is coincidental that CIA DCI Richard Helms rose to leadership in the Agency during the same years that I had a serious opportunity to move from the non-professional to the professional ranks of the Agency: 1966 - 1969. Just before Helms, Admiral William Raborn served the Agency as DCI. Raborn had become Director of CIA by April 28, 1965 and served until June 30, 1966. Helms served as Raborn's deputy from April 1965 until June 30, 1966. As a historical footnote, it was under Helms' leadership as DCI that I applied and was accepted into the Career Training Program (CTP) and had my tour in Latin America as a CIA Spy Manager.

Career Training Program (CTP)

During the summer of 1968, I made my move to get Agency management to sponsor me to the CTP. I bluntly asked Mr. Bleeding Heart, aka Softheart, point blank "Am I going to have a career in the

Agency or not?" I was brave enough to pose the question because I had run out of funds for school.

When I returned from the FNC and I was searching for a job. Ms. High Heels set me up in an interview for my first quasi Counter Intelligence job in the Branch lead by Mr. Bleeding Heart. He hired me but made no other promises. I knew he would do whatever he could to help me. I told him that I had run out of money for my college education and that getting into the CTP would provide an alternate solution so that I would be able to stay in the agency. Mr. Bleeding Softheart agreed to help me get into the Program because he thought I was an outstanding employee who deserved to become a Case Officer. He followed through on my behalf and I was admitted into the CT Program.

In the fall of 1969, the Agency appointed me to CTP. I was an internal candidate for the CTP because I was sponsored by an operational division, whereas most of the trainees were from outside of the Agency. Generally, when a person like me is sponsored as an internal, he or she returns to the component-sponsoring unit. For this reason, I knew I would return to the Division then lead by William Broe. Both he and Bleeding Heart served as two of my godfathers during this period. I was one of the first in the history of the CTP to actually get accepted into the training without a college degree. Therefore, I was one of the first to complete the Program without a college degree. I make a big deal about this accomplishment because the Agency regulations did not specifically require a college degree, so I used the loophole to make my opportunistic case to Mr. Bleeding Heart.

I completed the training and became a Case Officer, twelve years after joining the CIA. The training was very important to me because I had wanted to get it for years. In reality, I had deeply wanted it since I was 12 years old but did not know it then. Without the CTP, there was really not much of a chance for me to be a Case Officer even though there are Case Officers who do not "go through the complete training program."

The training consisted of three parts:

1) Training and practical experiences in working in the different Directorates of the Agency.

2) Extensive training in both the intelligence and espionage enterprises.

3) Para-military training including an overseas exercise.

My training experiences in secret para-military matters, which is a major part of Covet Action (CA) intelligence operations, turned out to be a most significant, and difficult adventure for me. First, I did not want to even take the rigorous para-military training. I had heard that this part of CA was going to be phased out soon, so I didn't want to waste my time. Boy, had I been mis-informed! This type of paramilitary CA, now called terrorism or guerrilla warfare remained, for sure. Based on my faulty thinking, I really had to focus in order to measure up since I was not a "jock" type. Para-military training required great effort like getting traditional special forces military training.

The overall CT program provided professional employees with advanced intelligence training, giving us an in-depth knowledge of the entire intelligence process from collection through processing and production. The CTP training enabled trainees to be prepared to work as both Case Officers and Intelligence Officers. I make a big deal about calling us Case Officers or Spy Mangers and not Intelligence Officers or "Agents". It is in this training where the rubber meets the road so I still like to distinguish us from the public perception of who and what a 'spy' is and does. Case Officers manage the spies, agents, and assets. You can quickly see why calling us Spy Managers works, right? You might say Case Officers are spy managers, or the colloquial "spy masters."

Getting the assignment in the DO meant I would be a Case Officer and for me no other option mattered. The graduates of CTP serve in management positions in any one of the four Agency Directorates. As a former DO internal CTP trainee, it was logical for me to return and serve in the Clandestine Services or work in the Directorate of Operations (DO) as some of us prefer to say. After completing general training that represented experiences in each of the directorates, we were given interim assignments in various Divisions and Branches in the DO before beginning the long part of the course that included the intensive intelligence operations, including Para-Military (PM) training. Note that PM used to be guerrilla warfare training but now everyone knows it as terrorism.

Early in my Agency work, I had two heroes who had graduated from the CTP, then called the Junior Officer Training (JOT) program-- Everett Plant and Evil Win. They were among the first African American graduates of the Program. I knew about these two, but had not heard of nor met Justice Arrow until much later in our lives. According to the record, Justice Arrow graduated from the JOT in 1957 and was one of the first Black Case Officer in CIA history.

All three of these Black Case Officers had come from outside of the Agency. We called such career trainees from the outside, "externals." I was from the inside, so was an "internal." To be an "internal" was more the exception than the rule. I was not the first Black internal. Other Blacks such as George Hockey and Cedric Roberts made the CTP before me. However, I was only the tenth African American to become a Case Officer in CIA.

76

As far as interesting statistics and information on my CTP class, we did one item worth mentioning. Three of the 26 members of the class had five children; two besides myself. Jack Devine and Chuck Enwrong had five children. Jack and I did not get too close during the training, but Chuck and I did. This happened in part because we were both internals. Chuck had actually worked directly for Helms. Because of that relationship we bonded. He, like me, was "an older person" who received an opportunity to get into the CTP.

At one point during the Career Training Program, in 1969, William Blee, then Chief of the Near East Division in the DO, lectured the our CTP class. I noticed that he gave the class the "look over" before beginning his presentation. That was my tip off that a person from a different culture is scouting the room to ensure that there are no Black folks present because they are going to do or say something wrong about Blacks. Since I don't jump out with the dark skin saying that I am a Black man, Mr. Blee was safe, or so he thought. So during the presentation he claimed as fact that OMITTED, OMITTED did not culturally accept Blacks.

I think the unfortunate event of Mr. Blee's speech above illustrates what I call the plight of the "light skinned" Negro who gets that exceptional opportunity to challenge ignorance. So, the experience has a dual connotation. It allows people like me to get the opportunity to challenge the beliefs of people like Blee while I get that inner satisfaction knowing even being a light-skinned there are advantages. Even though I don't have the dark skin, I still get the opportunity to confront those who make these serious cultural errors when their ancestors are the perps that created us light skinned Blacks.

My classmates, who knew I wouldn't let Mr. Blee's comment go unchallenged, looked around and toward me waiting for my reaction. I chose my timing and remembered my humiliation from high school. I also remembered my rejection by the Office of Communications (OC).

77

Both memories flashed through my mind and I could not let Blee's comments go unchallenged. I had proof in the form of personal experience that differed from his stated belief which I knew was inaccurate. I wanted this experience to be a "win" for me this time and not an unresolved emotional downer.

I politely asked Blee, "What is the evidence?"

He said, "It's the experience of the Agency that the Russians and Chinese don't respond well to Blacks."

I suggested that since there were no Agency Black Case Officers dealing with the Chinese and Russians, this couldn't possibly have ever happened. He backed down and I had notched up one small victory. Later, I learned that one of the incidents that he mentioned had nothing to do with a Black Case Officer not being wanted by an African agent. In reality the story involved a white case officer with an African who blocked the appointment of a Black non-professional who was getting the assignment. It had nothing to do with the Chinese or the Russians or any other foreigners. It was simply his own misconception.

I love my country, the United States of America, and would do anything within my power to protect its interests. Though I am now telling my story many years later and some 25 years after leaving the Agency, light bulb moments happened throughout my career and even now change my understanding of the truth about the USA. These epiphanies enable me to see and understand the truth about certain intelligence activities just a little differently than when I was actually going through the CIA period of my life. My understanding of CIA intelligence operations, especially Covert Action intelligence operations, have significantly changed while also becoming part of the Osborne Ultimatum. In short the Osborne Ultimatum asks the US Government to reduce if not eliminate Covert Action intelligence operations since there is little to no evidence that any of the dirty tricks achieve any genuine positive objectives.

I acquired a significant enlightenment on CA while I was still a long way from being a Spy Manager. In other words, when I was in the CIA learning about CA, I had not evolved my thoughts and paradigm to what it is today, so my writing about events in the past of course reflects my current thinking with the benefit of hindsight. Even though, I have attempted to keep the history in perspective I definitely have amended the events to reflect my thinking. So with that understanding, let me begin adding and weaving in the facts about CA that led to my paradigm shifts as well. One significant shift had to do with one of my favorite activities that I call identifying trigger words that have impact in risk communications especially with a person like me.

The first trigger word that I want to deal with is "slave." I seldom use it except to refer to an institution or a person's state of mind. I call the people who came to the United States America from Africa either "Africans" or stolen people because most of them had nothing to do with their relocation and assignment of bondage. My concept of Blacks or African Americans is an ethnic identity of the descendants of the stolen people. With this enlightenment my story has greater meaning and significance. I even dare to express the point that these descendants from the "stolen people" are the true heroes of U.S.A. history. I use the phrase "stolen people" to counter the use of the term 'slaves.' I feel it better characterizes the true heritage of the people from Africa who suffered in and endured the institution of slavery, especially since the institution of slavery in the USA is a unique cultural experience that was only found in the USA. Please note in my world no form of slavery equals nor matches the horror of slavery in the USA. Also in my mind's eye, slavery is a state of mind and the descendants of the stolen people did not have to accept the concept

79

even though they suffered the penalties and consequences of the institution of slavery.

Trigger words like slavery and descendants of the stolen people enabled me to postulate a continuing role for the descendants of the stolen people to force the Government and country to live up to the high ideals of human rights guaranteed in the laws of the USA. Besides using the concept of the descendants of the stolen people, I also modified the way I thought about the founding fathers, the men who made the original laws of the United States. It is both ironic that the descendants of the stolen people continue to serve as a persistent irritation in the society, functioning like sand in the oyster that makes the pearl. The pearl in this case is equal rights and human rights. This irritation enables the USA to live up to the high ideals of human and civil rights written into the laws of the country. This reality happened even though humans known as "land owners" at that time wrote the laws. They wrote amazing laws but unfortunately they had personality flaws that created and perpetuated cultural discrimination and segregation.

These Founding Fathers, as they are known, wrote the laws that only landowners could vote. The world knows there were others in the country at the time who were not land owners, including other descendants of Europeans, Africans born in the USA, and Native Americans. The homelands of the latter cultural group had been ruthlessly taken. There are "sins of omission" in our history books about the character flaws of the founding fathers. It remains a weakness of our education system. On the other hand, the parallel thoughts of the descendents of the stolen people in this US environment of injustice thrive. These descendents continue to press for changes and improvements in human rights and equal treatment.

Note I do not speak of Black history, as such, because everyone in the United States of America shares in the reality. When the

Constitution was written giving citizens these human rights, the authors themselves did not practice what they wrote. Unfortunately, I did not learn about this when I studied in school but I know it now. It is amazing and even astonishing that the founders who were landowners did not include the non-landowners in the right to vote. Only those who owned land voted, period. The landowners at the time *discriminated* against persons who did not own land and could not vote, including women. This preamble leads into some very weighty and interesting concepts necessary to understanding the intelligence industry. It helps explain how I initially learned details on Covet Action intelligence operations and helps the following discussion which is based on revelations of my own 20/20 hindsight.

Covert Action Operations

For me, the Agency has been one great big Covert Action (CA) organization. Those of us who conducted Foreign Intelligence (FI) and Counter Intelligence (CI) operations generally fared less well than those Case Officers who did the flashier CA operations. I will explain CA operations and list some of the more infamous operations so that you get a feel for them. First, the CA operations generally fail. When they become public, they are known by their "operations" name. By the way, my assessment of the Agency as a CA organization has been modified somewhat according to some of the younger Case Officers that I am meeting. They say that CA still has considerable value but "numbers and recruitments" tend to be the prevailing management agenda or evaluation criteria without any relevance to the quality of the recruits. To me, not all spies are of equal value.

When the Agency was formed in 1947, Covert Action operations were placed under the National Security Council with a carefully phrased "catchall: clause (Section 102(d)(5)), which provided the CIA

81

shall: perform such other functions and duties related to intelligence affecting the national security as the National Security Council may from time to time direct."

I took this to mean that Clark Clifford believed that since CA operations were not mentioned specifically, they would be separate and distinct from the normal activities of the CIA. He expected them to be limited in scope and purpose - thus the importance of the limiting language, affecting national security. Clifford expressed his concerns about Covert Action operations in 1987 and 1988 when he testified before the House and Senate. "If we are to continue with [covert operations] and gain any benefit from them, we must find a way to keep them consistent with the principles and institutions of the Constitution and our foreign policy." If we determine that this cannot be done, then I say we are better off without covert activities entirely than with them out of control. Although Clifford was not necessarily against covert action, many of my fellow case officers and I agree that there should be tighter controls such as consulting the President and Congress when planning to conduct Covert Action intelligence operations.

As I read Clifford's perceptions on CA, I decided that his opinions are very similar to mine. Thus, his CA opinions can serve as backdrop for my perceptions and positions on CA. As a matter of fact, Clifford's opinion serves as documentation for some of the historical events during my Agency experiences especially when I was countering Libyan intelligence activities.

Without doubt, Covert Action intelligence operations involve interference with another country's internal affairs. Allen Dulles said "There is, as far as I know, only one certain rule in international relations. Interference by one country in the internal affairs of another causes resentment. It is sure to produce a result exactly the opposite of that intended. We must not build barriers between ourselves and a third world, namely, the world which may practice a measure of state socialism."

Even though Clifford and Dulles have other positions on issues I don't embrace still I buy into their thoughts about CA; due to hindsight and my knowledge of multiple examples of so-called Agency failures. For me, if we had listened to and followed the true meaning of these guiding philosophies that shaped the CIA into the organization it is today, we would not be in the trouble we are in today. However, let's take another look at the system. CA has been working the way the system wanted. CA is working for them but not for the average citizen.

Two per cent of the population controls the other 98 per cent of the wealth. Those citizens should question and demand their political leaders keep the CIA in check and compel the truth to come out.

The 2%ers decided to ease up on the stiff-necked discrimination in the late 1940's. At least my readings from Clark Clifford's biographical material suggested this. I discovered that he considered President Truman's Executive Order 9981 in the same historical context as Jackie Robinson's breakthrough, reducing discrimination in baseball in 1947. The Executive Order 9981, dated July 27, 1948 states "It is hereby declared to be the policy of the President that there shall be equality of treatment and opportunity for all persons in the armed services without regard to race, color, religion, or national origin." I found it most fascinating that Clark Clifford, publicly and privately, endorsed Truman's minority stratagem. That is, Clifford wrote that he had recommended that President Truman "go as far as he feels he possibly could in recommending measures to protect the rights of minority groups." and he was known by those of us in the agency as saying the same thing in personal and private moments. The civil rights message was far more than a campaign stratagem: it committed the Democratic party to a historic enterprise from which there was no turning back --

the quest for equal rights for all Americans. At the same time, the identification of the Democrats with the struggle for civil rights would be the primary factor that drove the South into the Republican camp in most subsequent Presidential elections.

The above examples of changes in the prior "system" by Truman and Clifford in my opinion serve as models for further sweeping changes in the system. Therefore, as the saying goes, there is hope.

I disliked Covert Action or "CA" as it was called among my colleagues. CA has been a government policy decision that is implemented in the intelligence business when all diplomatic activity fails. It is generally a last resort before open war and fighting. We learned to speak of CA as "the step before war," in our Agency Career Training (CTP). I defined CA in three levels of secrecy:

1. White = identifiable as a US action/issue.

2. Gray = plausible denial by US politicians.

3. Black = invisible hand of the U.S./always denied no matter what.

The use of Covert Action in U.S. policy has been continuously debated now for decades. I doubt that they will cease and desist. I knew deep down how Covert Action was being used, adversely affecting the global majority, but I did not do enough to enter into a discussion about how it could be changed. I guess that's why I am still around, still working toward that dream. A peek into my destiny as some of my friends will say will definitely let you know that I am still on the job.

One reason I am writing this book is to explore my desire to change US Government proclivities. We use CA in solving problems instead of obtaining and efficiently directing more agents to collect the truth. The history of CA is a consistent history of failed CA operations more than anything else. Failed CA ops are what most people hear about. I thought, it may be helpful to write about Covert Action in connection with the Agency leaders during and after these Covert Action operations. The repercussions, or blow-back of covert action are public concerns, and even that concern is "handled." Remember, I am one of the detractors. I have sprinkled in a little counter terrorism from my experiences as well.

Other Agency outcasts who have gone public, Phil Agee and John Stockwell, had issues with Covert Action intelligence operations. Victor Marchetti and John D. Marks express sentiments about Agency CA close to my own impressions of the value and end results of CA operations. On one hand I did not attempt to change the pre-eminence of CA in Agency operations. But though I avoided confrontation of CA intelligence operations during my service, I did re-examine them from the side lines because deep down I knew how Covert Action was being used and still is used, adversely affecting people of color. Covert Action (CA) activities that used propaganda and other techniques to achieve intelligence objectives just did not play well with me. I have observed that many Covert Action and paramilitary activities of the Agency caused many of the problems with Congress and the American people. Because of this I built a world around me and others of similar thinking about counter intelligence and foreign intelligence collections. I had blinders on and refused to MEMBER OF A FOREIGN INTELLIGENCE SERVICEengage in covert action. These blinders caused me not to pursue activities of the CS which may have permitted me to be closer to Agency programs that have adversely impacted the civil rights movement.

The CIA began in 1947, ten years before I joined. Then it was the dawn of the grand era of Anti-Communism. I grew with the Agency and progressed as well.

I agree with recent comments on the Agency. That is, the CIA in the past two decades has in fact become an Agency so troubled and compromised that it seems to have created a culture of failure, manifested in the discovery of OMITTED and the Attack on America. I call the era of double agents "the years of the spies." My observations are based on my strong belief that CI deals with countering adversary intelligence activities of other governments and offensive HUMINT (Human Intelligence) operations against the USA, which includes turning our intelligence resources against us. A double agent is an intelligence agent or asset that also works for the other side.

Such a manifestation was Aldrich Ames. The Aldrich Ames scandal exploded in 1994. Revelations about Ames, being a double agent, who was the CIA's head of Soviet Counter Intelligence, destroyed the CIA's Eastern bloc operations. At least a dozen American agents were executed as a result of his treachery. This case was merely the worst of many operational failures from the 1980s onward. Other revelations showed that the CIA's 40-odd supposed spies in Cuba turned out to be double agents working for Castro. Agents were uncovered, arrested, tortured, or expelled in a number of countries around the world. Worse yet, hardly anyone in management was disciplined, let alone fired, as a result of these almost catastrophic failures.

My fight against Covert Action Intelligence operations may be traced to early in my intelligence career when I had a non-professional position. I valued my capacity to develop facts and information that prepared me and some others for the Agency Spy Manager and Counter Intelligence roles where we countered adversary intelligence activities. When the facts were sometimes used for Covert Action intelligence operations, I saw unsatisfactory returns with a lot of smoke and mirrors rather than tangible results. The best example -- which the whole world knows – is the intelligence failure of the Bay of Pigs, a failed invasion of Cuba. It is my opinion, the failure by the Agency to obtain extensive Counter Intelligence information on the Cubans that directly led to the aborted and utterly tragic operation.

In the public arena, often the discussion about Covert Action intelligence operations is tied to the war powers of the United States. In short, before a war the USA's CA operations are designed to circumvent and reduce the need to get Congress involved. CA operations, especially terrorist operations, delay, postpone and seldom eliminate the reasons for a shooting war that generally follows secret para-military warfare.

Therefore, CA intelligence operations infringed on the right of Congress to declare war. (U.S. Const. Art. I. Section 8,cl.11.) The Presidents of the United States and Congress continue the debate of "executive privilege" on a regular basis. If I had to make a decision, I would support a Congressional prohibition of all Covert Action intelligence operations without prior notice, consultation and approval for all uses of military force. Therefore, I would be a proponent of the American Civil Liberties Union's 1961 publication "Ending the Cold War at Home, Public Policy Report, Winter, 1991 (202) 544-1681.

I was trained to define terrorism as "secret para-military warfare between nation-states." However, today even non nation-states do terrorism, or do they? It follows that today one person's view of a terrorist is another person's revolutionary, freedom fighter or guerrilla warfare fighter depending on how nation-states want the public to perceive their propagandized message. I will continue to add insight into Covert Action terminologies throughout my story along with some anecdotal stories. So hang in here, please.

87

During a CTP interim assignment in the WHD (Western Hemisphere Division), I found yet another mentor in Jack Bates, my supervisor there. During that assignment in one of the WHD (Western Hemisphere Division) branches, Bates used my research and CI skills to assist him counter Soviet intelligence activities in one of the Latin American countries. Further, under his guidance, I also supported field efforts at recruiting Soviets. After the interim assignment I returned to CTP and completed the training. Fortunately, I excelled in the CTP long intelligence operations, especially on the field exercises, even though my para-military training was not as strong. nevertheless, I did finish.

I was "wired" and hyped for the Agency training, but not ready for the reality of what I was learning firsthand in the jungle. I had prepared myself for the para-military training. I stopped smoking and lost 25 pounds. We got that mean and lean attitude for para-military training. After this phase of the training was over, I had a new attitude: I realized bluntly that the only person I had to count on was my God and maybe myself, certainly, no other human being.

As we walked through the jungle, one of my classmates, passed out, collapsing right there in the middle of the jungle. Some of my other classmates helped place him on a poncho. He looked as if he was dying. We huddled around. I was close to one of the instructors, so I asked him if he planned to call in a helicopter to med-e-vac the fallen student to be taken to a treatment facility.

The class instructor said he wasn't going to get anyone because he didn't know where we were either. I asked him, "Are you telling me that you're responsible for all of these people out here in the jungle and you don't know where you are?" Shockingly, he said that was true. I asked him what he was going to do. He said he'd send us out to scan the area for the rappel cliff and then we should come back to get the rest of the class. In the interim he would wait for the fallen classmate to regain consciousness.

Suddenly we heard a voice and we came upon this great big, seven-foot, military guy who had been waiting for us at the cliff. My classmate regained consciousness and was able to go on, so the military officer showed us to a ravine just before the rappel cliff. The officer jumped the ravine and had each of us do the same thing. He actually caught us with his big hands and long arms as we jumped. We all went to the point and began rappelling. The same classmate, who collapsed and blacked out before, did it again, this time while he was rappelling. I remember this picture of him hanging there with everyone, including the instructors, just watching. I saw water dripping off the mountain onto him.

I couldn't stand it. After I heard the instructor responsible for my life saying he didn't have any way to help us, I decided I knew why things went wrong in Vietnam. It was common for para-military operations to go wrong. I had developed this bias against para-military operations because it is part of "Covert Action" operations. Some of these same instructors had played significant roles in the Vietnam War. These were the people who were responsible for the Vietnam mess and all the other Agency para-military mistakes. I researched the intelligence-based programs and found that no covert action intelligence programs ever worked. The only Agency clandestine training that was of any real value was in trade-craft techniques, which I called the "magic." Trade-craft was the secret stuff that enabled me to keep others from knowing what I was actually doing as a Case Officer directing agents and informants.

By the time I had my CTP training, CA intelligence operations continued to take on different appearances. Even though covert action intelligence operations were conducted allegedly to prevent wars, they were in fact undeclared wars. Vietnam was a CA operation until it was declared a war. It is terrorism at its best.

Perhaps one of the best examples of a change in covert action intelligence operations was in the old traditional placement operations. That is, a Case Officer recruited and used newspaper reporters to place stories, propaganda and even lies. However, as the years passed, Congress shut down these types of covert action intelligence operations. CIA no longer used newspaper reporters in this traditional manner. When the law changed the CIA had to terminate actually recruiting journalists.

As I was acquiring more insights into intelligence, I still was using my knowledge from my thirteen years of practical experience in CIA, including the one overseas tour in the Far Northern Country. Mr. Broe turned out to be a key godfather in my Agency experience. Through his leadership, the Agency both sponsored me to have the CTP appointment and then to take courses at the American University of Washington, D.C.

I engineered the opportunity with the blessings of management so that I completed and earned my undergraduate college degree. Curiously, the government could pay only for courses as long as we did not connect it with my earning the degree. By selecting the college where my prior credits were accepted, I was able to get the financial aid and degree. During the sojourn in full time school, I received full pay, no work on the job, tuition paid and books paid. What a deal! With the absence of a job and duty work, I was able to allocate full time to focusing on my 11 courses at The American University and graduate with honors the Political Science Honor Society, the Pi Sigma Alpha, Beta Psi chapter on May 28, 1971.

A little history of the Osborne family with The American University is in order. In my opinion, The American University was geared for white success and Blacks had little if any support infrastructure in the university. Fortunately, I did not need any, but in hindsight it might have been helpful. Blacks at American University in 1970 were few in number but no outward signs of discrimination existed. Nevertheless, the University would not let me register as a student in the Foreign Affairs Institute. I had to settle for taking courses in the Institute and earning my degree from the School of Political Science, with 9 of my 11 courses in Latin American affairs.

However, history has a great way of providing pay back. In addition to completing college, The American University awarded me membership in the political science honor society that I already mentioned. Some years later as one might will it, two of our daughters, De Levay Cabrina Osborne and Monique Therese Osborne attended The American University. One of them, De Levay, even registered and received her degree from the same Institute that rejected me before the University would allow a Black person to get a degree from the Institute. You will remember, I could take courses from the Institute but not graduate.

After returning to work in the WHD (Western Hemisphere Division) in one of the branches I had an experience that I will never forget. One day this nameless C/O working for the C/LAD, had the nerve to invoke the name of the LA Division Chief, William Broe and ask me to take an assignment. He actually threatened me if with repercussions if I did not accept the assignment to Vietnam. He said, "Mr. Broe may want to discuss the turn down with you."

I repeated my answer, "No" and the subject was never brought up again. The irony of the above experience with the guy representing Mr. Broe eventually motivated me to seek another educational experience. The effort to ascertain my willingness to serve in Vietnam came just after I had completed the CTP.

It wasn't long before a real offer for a real assignment in a Latin American Country (LAC) came to me. I was given the opportunity to go full time to learn Spanish before going to the LAC.

When I completed the Spanish course, I did not score as well as I had wanted and told the professor of Spanish that I wanted to do better. I had scored a 2 plus but I knew I needed a 3 level or even better for such an assignment. So I requested an extension of my study so I could at least get a 3-plus. I heard through the grapevine that Shackley and his new people did not like me requesting an extension of the Spanish language training so I could improve my knowledge, but I did it anyway. By extending my time in Washington before leaving Headquarters for the assignment, the Agency had to send another spy manager on Temporary Duty to fill in for me until I arrived at the LAC. So I started the language course again to assure my fluency. The instructor assured management that I had the ability and would definitely improve once I was in the environment of Spanish-speaking people.

As events unfolded, the Spanish instructor and one of my fellow language students became engaged and we had a class party. Some of the class members, including spouses and key persons from the Division, went to the party. Ted Shackley and his wife attended, as did Rose and I. We still had not received the official notice to pack out and get our tickets for the assignment.

Shortly after entering the party, Rose and I had an opportunity to meet Shackley and his wife again. Rose took advantage of the situation. Now I can elaborate on her motive more than I realized at the time. Rose and I discussed this event many times because, it appeared to me, Rose rather boldly challenged Shackley given his powerful status in the Agency. Being a strong woman supporting me, she blossomed in this moment in our history with the Agency.

Rose bluntly asked Shackley whether we should pack out or not. Shackley looked taken aback by the question, but when he looked at his wife, he knew he had to say something. So, he said reluctantly, "Yes, I guess so." After that, we were excited and really enjoyed the party. So, this is how Shackley reluctantly concurred and approved my assignment as a Case Officer to the Latin American country (LAC). I owe a great debt of gratitude to my wife Rose for courageously confronting Shackley.

For three weeks, Rose and I waited while management confirmed Shackley's decision for us to pack out. Shackley ran a tight operation had the mid-level management scared. They wouldn't confront or challenge anything he said or did. Shackley ruled by intimidation and the managers accepted it without a word of dissension.

I have told you about my graduate education in the CTP, my undergraduate work to earn my degree in political science and my Spanish language training. I also had other training experiences, which I think contributed to my education while at the CIA.

Chapter 7:

Tour in Latin American Country (LAC)

By late in 1971, I had graduated from American University with a degree in Political Science from the School of Government Service. I was one of four Black Case Officers in the WHD (Western Hemisphere Division) and ready for a second assignment abroad, once as a clerk in the mail and now as a Case Officer. So this time I would be performing more than clerical work in the mail room. Rather than wrapping packages in the mail-room, I would be the real thing -- a CIA Case Officer in the field as a spy supervisor. My childhood dream had finally come true after lots of work, sacrifice, guidance and luck.

While I was away from the Agency and assigned to the American University taking the 11 courses I needed to graduate, the Latin American Division changed its name to the Western Hemisphere Division (WHD). Mr. Broe, my godfather, was gone, having retired, however I still had several persons with godfather status.

One of them was Jack Bates who re-appeared in my life right on time. He briefed me about the new Chief of the WH Division, one Theodore Shackley who had brought his own cadre of assistants, including Hank Hammerhead as Deputy Chief. I didn't know Hammerhead but knew his girlfriend who eventually became his wife.

She and I had worked together in the Branch after returning to work from college.

Shackley neither liked nor respected me. It was nothing personal because it is my take that he only had a very few Case Officers he liked at all. I eventually got to learn more about Shackley. I considered him a sinister man, almost a common thug, but one of the "sharpest knives in the drawer," as some of us say. The WH Division required that I take what was called the full Spanish course in preparation for this second assignment abroad in the Latin American Country (LAC) but this time as a spy manger. I was very motivated because after the briefing by Godfather Bates I also knew I needed to be sure I mastered the language. My attitude about the score had been influenced by godfather Bates statement that Headquarters expected me to recruit someone once I arrived at the new post and this particular person did not speak any English. That is, Bates told me that I was to handle a very sensitive asset for a while after arriving in the LAC. There I was to recruit him so that he would work for the United States without his country knowing it. In the espionage enterprise, I was to "recruit him" without his own intelligence service knowing it. Such a recruitment is called a(n) OMITTED penetration. With the heads up briefing given me by my mentor Bates, I knew my primary task was to recruit what we call a foreign language speaking "third country asset." My assignment was to continue hand holding the asset for a short period after I arrived with the explicit intent of recruiting him. That would mean I had to gain his confidence, convince him to betray his country and work for the United States government.

This was a genuine Counter Intelligence requirement, since the United States would be in a position to learn secrets about the friendly country's internal security operations and activities without compromising friendly relations with the country and its intelligence

95

service. In some circles, the person I was to recruit might have been considered a double agent. That may be so for me, the challenge of the language was almost more than what I wanted to handle, but added to the task of recruiting an intelligence officer from another country, I knew I would really have my hands full.

In the espionage enterprise, we use strict definitions for an agent and an asset. An asset is not necessarily controlled, whereas there is a defined degree of control on spies that are agents. Therefore, the person I recruited was described as an asset because both Headquarters and myself knew that he was not 100% under U.S. control. An asset that is not under control predetermines the trust that is afforded to the person. Thus less control, less trust and more precautions are required in performing Case Officer work.

WHD Assignment 72-74

The CIA gave us official orders and assigned us to the Latin American Country (LAC) from 1972 through 1974, after my supervisors got the word from Shackley. Our family was ready to travel immediately to the LAC. Rose and I with the five children now made up our family: De Levay, Monique, Leutrell II, Natasha Inez and Carlton X. Natasha Inez Osborne, number three daughter was born May 14, 1967. Carlton Xavier Osborne, number two son, was born July 12, 1969.

I went through an extensive Agency process to get Thomas Motley, my youngest brother, included as a dependent family member, but he did not travel with us. Instead he stayed in New York City at Columbia University, where he was well on his way to becoming an attorney like our other brother, Frank Motley, III; Thomas graduated from Harvard Law School in 1979:
http://www.dccourts.gov/dccourts/docs/DCSC_Bio_Motley.pdf

Frank graduated from Columbia Law School in 1979:

http://info-p.law.indiana.edu/sb/page/normal/1496.html

All five (5) of us arrived in the LAC and I immediately took up residence in a beautiful hotel. I secured my Volkswagen station wagon from customs and eventually went to work. Rose and the children got everyone enrolled in elementary and middle school. Fortunately there were American-run schools in the LAC, so settling in went exceptionally well.

Before I get into what happened at the LAC and especially the Station operations, let me set the stage with some basic understanding of the "Espionage Enterprise" (EE). One needs to understand both the roles and the nature of the EE. Unclassified information housed in the leaders of the foreign country or nation states does not present any challenge. U.S. State Department employees, assigned overseas in the US Embassy, collect this information through routine duties and exchanges with officials of the host country and other foreigners. This non-protected information is unclassified. That is the "overt" nature of the Embassy officials' jobs. The corresponding protocol for protected information is sometimes similar to the overt protocol. The secret part of the US government requirement lies in wanting to know especially the protected information. Some may use the word "covert" referring to secret information and the term covert gets used as a synonym for secret, but don't confuse it with the EE operation: Covert Action Intelligence operations.

I went to work in the LAC and began an extensive settling in process taking over the agents and assets from the person who had gone to the LAC to perform my work until I completed language training. We refer to the assignment as Temporary Duty (TDY). Once my task of taking over the agents from this TDY person was completed, the TDYer left and I was ready to do my work. By this time, I had begun moving in social circles and started developing a wide network of social contacts from the local as well as the foreign population.

This Latin American Country (LAC) where I went was considered by many to be a "safe" place to send Black Case Officers. All four of the Black Case Officers in the Division eventually served in this same LAC. A part of the belief why this LAC was OK for Blacks coincided with management's views on the citizens in this country. Many of the citizens of this LAC had a rich immigration of the "stolen people" from Africa, just like it was in the US of A. For the record, I stopped using the term "slave" because with my Nubian mind I think and believe one that is stolen is different than one that truly is a slave. So the question to ponder is whether the Africans that were stolen from Africa coped the slave institution mentality or not? Thus, I preferred to use the term "stolen people" instead for my African ancestors.

There was good and bad news in the assignment. First, the good news was that Horacio Jones and I were in the same country working OMITTED. What a highpoint for me! Our careers had crossed several times, but never in the same place and same Station. Horacio and I continued our friendship and often talked about his significant achievements, which I admired. We met often and discussed a variety of topics.

Horacio once told me that his achievements were the direct result of his personality type that led him to near mental collapse and threatened his personal relationships, including those with his family. His ability to lie and yet be believed by others; to work impossible hours to the neglect of his responsibilities in his personal life; and the ability to manipulate superiors, associates and enemy agents made him an ideal OMITTED. Unfortunately, his successes masked the consequences of his personality traits. With much help from his religious training and participation in various self-help programs, Horacio came to terms with his deficiencies. I am sharing his experiences in this book to help others.

Now, to the bad news. To my chagrin, I encountered some serious discrimination from a person I call a "Yurugo" behaving co-optee." Since he did not trace his roots to Europe to most I can make him is s co-opted member of the Ego centric persons who lack their female chromosomes. This person was named Joe Lee and worst yet, Lee was the Chief of Station (COS) and as such he held the senior Agency official position abroad in a country. My supervisor answered to this COS who was assisted by the Deputy Chief of Station, Frank Espousa.

Joe Lee was a towering six-foot, four-inch, Japanese American. I was under his thumb for the entire two-year tour. He was an insensitive person for sure. The story of Joe Lee was that he was the same person who in the early 1960's had dogged my steps while I was in the Far Northern European Country. Lee was the very same person who had objected to my having had operational opportunities to "build rapport" and cultivate relationships with foreigners, and especially with Soviet KGB and GRU officers. I found out that this was a part Joe's resentment toward me. Regardless, Joe was proud of the fact that he had been the very same person who had turned down my operational requests when I was in the Far Northern European Country. His wife, Beverly Lee, was also a narrow thinker. This background on Joe and Beverly Lee helped set the stage for the evaluation challenges that eventually came about during my tour in LAC.

Although I had the same general credentials as other Case Officers in the Station, I was the junior officer because this was my first tour as an operations officer even though I had been overseas once before. Having more than one tour really enables a Case Officer to get the better selection of agents and definitely enables one to get better assignments, and to work against the harder intelligence targets. Because I was a junior officer, Joe Lee had ample opportunity to ensure that I received the lowest work assignments, the dirty details and limited opportunities to perform. Sometimes it was difficult to sort out genuine professional bias versus "Yurugu supremacy" because " one must fit a cultural mold" in order to reach the top as an operations officers in the Agency.

When I first arrived, I took over relatively weak operations and managed to get oriented and improve my language rapidly. I worked hard at the language, especially with the assets who did not speak English. There were no hard targets when I arrived in the Latin American Country (LAC).

My operations were relegated to the less than glorious work for Case Officers. I was the junior Case Officer at the Station so from the start and thereafter I was assigned the routine and mundane tasks of the Station. I was the Station technical referent, which meant I handled the storage of Station technical goods and facilitated contacts with the Tech types during visits.

Of course during the first year, I went to work on the recruitment task that Bates had told me about. This was one of the biggest achievements I ever made in the Espionage Enterprise. For the record however, it only led to some real challenges in getting a reasonable evaluation for the first year abroad at the LAC Station. I also was faced with handling a couple of low level operations against the communist students. These tasks enabled me to perform as the Station's tech referent. I assisted the other Case Officers by providing technical support to their operations though I got neither credit nor responsibility for leading the operations. From a leadership perspective, generally Case Officers lead and take charge of their agents and operational tasks. At this time, the technical operations were telephone and audio technical operations. Though I did not have the agents nor the operation, I was given the operational experience to interface with the true technical technician and the Station Case Officers.

As I have stated already there were no hard targets when I arrived. However, given the operational environment, I still was cut in and controlled the asset that was used, while coordinating the work of the Agency technical professional who did the actual technical installation.

During that first year, I successfully accomplished a very significant task in that I recruited an intelligence officer of a third country to work for the CIA. This was an interesting development because the agent was a member of a(n) OMITTED intelligence service on diplomatic duty in this Latin American country. He agreed to our arrangement because he agreed to work against a mutual target and wanted his country to continue receiving favorable relationships with the United States. Through our arrangement, he could further his aspirations.

For a new Case Officer, recruiting someone is a giant step, but to recruiting an intelligence officer, which we called a(n) OMITTED penetration of a country's intelligence infrastructure, was noteworthy. I felt great because Jack Bates was very proud of my accomplishment. Unfortunately, I never saw him again. He had been there in my life at the right time to serve as a mentor and help me so that I had the opportunity to perform well in this Latin American Country (LAC). This is something I thank him for and will never forget.

I would begin my work at 7 am each work day. The Chief of Station, Joe Lee demanded that the Case Officers be in our seats when he came through the building in the morning. If I had an agent meeting, it had to be before or after the time I was expected at the office. That was that. We all did it without exception.

Hence, anyone watching activities of the Station Case Officers would know that the adversary intelligence can take a break between 6:45 am and 7:45 am because no agent meetings would be taking place. Anyway, that was just a thought on poor leadership, since behavioral patterns are obviously quickly assessed. I had dreamed of being a case Officer for so long. I envisioned what it would be like when I was assigned overseas before at the Far Northern Country. My idealized imagination had not included an adversarial supervisor like Lee.

Joe Lee happened to be the single person who gave me my most serious challenge in the chain of command. It was a serious adversary relationship with discrimination struggles despite the fact he was himself Japanese American. Unfortunately, the man died a painful death and some people who thought him to be their adversary were glad he suffered. Regardless of a person's attitude about Joe Lee, his memory lives in my mind and also in the minds of some others who he did not like him for one reason or another.

Joe Lee had profound impact on my career: two evaluations lowered my profile making me stay in grade eleven for years. Lee did not believe I had the necessary talents to be an effective operations officer. Joe felt that I got through the entire system easier than he did. Now let me try to ascertain from a historical perspective what he had a struggle with.

Joe's thinking was a little strange, but understandable. He had to accept a temporary duty person to perform my job while I received adequate language training. He had little if any choice in permitting my assignment in Latin American Country. Before coming to the LAC, I was offered a choice of two assignments in two different countries. I chose my own medicine because I wanted a greater opportunity to perform in operations in this LAC.

I did not possess those social graces that he had striven his entire life to attain. Mr. Lee dressed well, spoke well, wrote well, and for most observers he was impeccable as a leader of a(n) OMITTED station. The flaws in Lee were the result of my being almost the complete opposite of him. I did not have the social skill that he possessed. I had the experiences and capability to act independently and not be tied to a prescribed role.

I did not speak the same as him. I could jump from street English to standard American English within the same paragraph when talking to him or anyone else. My vocabulary was nowhere as strong as his, but my capabilities with the resources within gave me the competitive edge that annoyed him. I did not dress as well because my cash resources and attitude at the time were on other non-material things. My funds went into family. My attention was first to wife and children. All other actions, attitudes and emotional directions came thereafter. Being the lowest person on the officer totem pole I was always below Lee. As the children have said, "I was in the mustard and could not catch up."

My immediate supervisors were Larry Sulcz and Barry Roydan each for one year. They did not always support Mr. Lee's attitude about me; they both had their careers to protect and generally acquiesced to the whims of the iron-fisted boss, Joe Lee. Sulcz was the first supervisor to ever tell me that the big boss Joe had it in for me and I had to be careful. Roydan was the first supervisor to come out with it, bluntly. Barry Roydan said, "Mike, Joe is after you because you are Black."

At the Station, I worked hard at planning and organizing my clandestine and overt activities to make sure I did the very best job I could. Handling my caseload meant responding to the needs of my agents and informants. It is usually overseas that a case officer has opportunities for meeting agents and exchanging information and requirements.

Joe Lee saw me coming and used me up. Later that first year he threw hard assignments and near-impossible tasks at me in the hope that I would be preoccupied and not notice the unprofessional antics of my colleagues, who ran "phantom operations." The Agency also wanted me to avoid noticing the failure of Covet Action intelligence operations that had many negative results. One of my supervisor's assigned me the task of assisting him to discover the past activities of one of the Station case officers. Hence I witnessed and assisted in developing information that proved that several Case Officers conducted operational activities that did not exist.

I coined the term "phantom operations." These types of phantom operations included wrongful acts with and against agents. Some case officer lied about paying their agents. Also these very same case officers fabricated information from these agents to make the agents appear more valuable to the Agency than they really were. I could not help but notice the Agency use of and involvement in certain Covert Action activities to which I had strong objections. In fact, I worked alongside some of the same Case Officers who eventually became involved in Iran/Contra in later years in the early 1980s.

In 1973, CIA gave up pre-eminence in countering drugs and the Drug Enforcement Agency (DEA) absorbed the worldwide responsibility. This was during the transition of my first year at the LAC. Even then I knew that the United States government was one giant Covert Action intelligence program so it didn't make a big difference whether the activity is housed in the CIA or the DOD. Covert Action intelligence operations were the pre-eminent intelligence operation over two other types of intelligence operations. In short, they are preferred over Foreign Intelligence (FI) collection operations and Counter Intelligence operations. In Counter Intelligence, a foreign country's intelligence organization, like the CIA, attempts to obtain information from the United States government and the CIA is charged with countering that effort. So we had skills, called trade craft that we used against the adversary. Over the years, the activities of intelligence organizations grew larger, so much so that the CI arena also included countering drug traffickers and countering terrorists.

This transition and termination of CIA anti-narcotics activities was one of the lowest moments in my CIA experience. The White House ordered the CIA to get out of the business of trying to catch and neutralize drug traffickers. The stated reason was that the administration did not want CIA officials, agents and assets testifying in open court. I was skeptical of that reasoning but I accepted the decision and re-directed one of my finest agents, who had been doing an excellent job in fighting the drug dealers. I think the long-term consequences of that decision included the proliferation of drug trafficking in the United States today. My attitude on this topic reluctantly is not being covered in my memoirs because I plan to tell these stories about transnational drug enterprises in a separate book that I will write maybe sooner than later.

In this LAC, the internal police of the host government was treated like any other hostile intelligence service: we called and countered them as internal police hard targets. Remember, generally internal police organizations neither know they are perceived as nor operate like adversary intelligence organizations. Thus in this host country, the internal police also had the power to lock me up so my plans always included actions that would ensure my activities would escape police scrutiny. I always had cover for action.

I began the second year on the down side. The real downer pertains to my 2nd evaluation at the LAC Station. Barry Roydan, like my previous supervisor called me in to discuss my evaluation. Barry told me he had to lower it from Outstanding to Superior because Joe

Lee the Chief of Station refused to allow him to give me the outstanding. That's the story. Basically the results were that I would be re-assigned back to Washington for sure.

Yet, ironically, here is where fate kicks in and I get assigned as the Chief of the Central American Branch Counter Intelligence, chasing terrorists and countering adversary intelligence services around the world from a post in Washington while serving on a leadership team.

As my first year started ending, the operational environment improved. That is, low level and non-hard targets started to become hard targets, such as the Russians. As you recall, training involves mastering operations against hard targets like the Russians, Cubans, Chinese and the drug dealers. Since I was highly motivated, I was focused and knew where I wanted to end up during my actual first operational assignment abroad.

Thus by the end of the first year I had a(n) OMITTED agents which kept me very busy, especially because I had the only station OMITTED penetration into a third country intelligence service. By this time the OMITTED, and OMITTED started moving into the country and for me that meant more "targets" to go after; performing telephone taps on them allowed me to collect operational information. The OMITTED came in the next year, but we started with operations against the OMITTED.

Much of my work pertained to technical operations; I regularly received tech type visitors. We were planning and improving my technical operations. I had a "bug" on OMITTED. I had a bug and a tap on OMITTED. I had a tap on OMITTED. I had a tap on OMITTED. All these technical operations required tremendous quantities of support and resources, including assisting agents and assets.

The acquisition of an old worn out agent, who had been trained in China and Cuba, enabled me to get credit for the first audio tap against OMITTED. I also got credit for disseminating intelligence information from an audio tap. The staging and strategic planning for the technical operation was enormous, though it began at a regular agent meeting. However, first let me explain how I lucked out even getting the operation much less the opportunity to perform at an outstanding level.

This meeting came soon after I inherited the agent that I call Hernandez for my story. At this point I want to make it clear that using a person's real name could cause serious risk of that person being killed in some cases so at times I will use a cover name. One of the more senior Case Officers had been handling Hernandez, but that handler had to leave on a family emergency. Management decided to let me take over this former very high powered agent who was not quite out to pasture. I did a quick study and learned that Hernandez had been trained in para-military tactics in both China and Cuba. In short, Hernandez was a genuine terrorist who was no longer was practicing his trade but was still fully capable of doing so. He now was a OMITTED for OMITTED officials who had just arrived and opened the OMITTED in the LAC. So, in the trade I now had an agent who had access to a hard target.

My life as a Case Officer was destined for a quantum leap in excitement and high adventure. Hernandez showed up at the scheduled meeting and early into the meeting he casually showed me a key. It was a rather large and long key. It was over OMITTED. I asked him what was it for? I listened attentively as Hernandez was another one of those agents that did not speak any English. In hindsight, I can say my language skills again were paying off. I clearly understood when Hernandez answered me saying it was the key to OMITTED. It took me only a few seconds to advise Hernandez we had to schedule an emergency meeting in two hours because I naturally wanted to make a copy of the key, immediately. We agreed.

I probably broke some speed records but I went back to the Station with great excitement and secured the necessary equipment to prepare myself to meet with Hernandez to copy the key. Fortunately, my readiness paid off. Remember, I had been the Station's tech referent so I had firsthand knowledge of the equipment location and operation. I had even been involved in several training sessions where I used the key impression equipment.

I met with Hernandez at the precisely agreed upon time. Hernandez and I dutifully went to work copying the key, realizing it would open more than doors. Hernandez knew I was copying the key and that I would need his assistance when I planned to do something with it. However, we agreed that he would get more details after I had the go ahead to use the duplicate key. We cut the meeting short after reviewing details of our future planned and regular meetings. We both realized we just may have to be meeting a little more frequently to coordinate further.

I applied for and won approval from Washington to conduct an audio penetration into OMITTED. As is the case when something like this operation is taking place, there is a pervasive sense a big event is taking place. The COS and my superior, the Chief of Ops, Barry Roydan became just a little more involved. More than directive, they became more "hands on" with my operation. I didn't mind because I was naturally excited and looking forward to doing a significant mission and my first audio operation against OMITTED.

Within ten days, over 15 or more Headquarters personnel were involved in different capacities, some even showing up for the actual penetration operation. Everyone did their job including Hernandez. When the operation was complete OMITTED was fully "wired" for stereophonic sound and I was getting daily translations of events and activities of OMITTED. With the human source reporting especially from Hernandez, my OMITTED operation was rolling along smoothly. I was really busy, now handling a portfolio of OMITTED agents, including Hernandez.

One day a potentially startling report came to me, indicating OMITTED plans to open embassies in Latin America. I worked very hard to get the information ready for what we call an "Intel report." I was taking raw information from a technical operation and preparing it for electronic distribution to Headquarters. From there it was slated for dissemination to the Intelligence Community (IC), which includes the White House as an addressee. Everyone worked hard and the Intel report on OMITTED plans for opening embassies across the continent was disseminated. The tech info now became finished intelligence.

The successful audio operation took a significant position in the Agency history for the LA Division now had successfully prosecuted a technical operation producing finished intelligence. Of course, everyone especially those of us at the LAC Station were happy. The fact that I could take the glory for the operation and now for the dissemination, thrilled me. I knew I was in for an outstanding evaluation. As a matter of fact Mr. Lee, the COS got his promotion in part because of events at the Station. Naturally, my activities, especially the OMITTED operation, played a major role in the success of the Station.

Unfortunately, I don't know if I was the first Case Officer to complete such an achievement, but I do know I was the first Black Case Officer to get credit for producing a finished intelligence report from a technical operation. I have also been told that this operation in 1974 was the first ever for any Case Officer, as far as I know. My being a Black American just added another layer of uniqueness to this accomplishment. So the historical fact is this: I was the first Black Case Officer to prepare and have the Agency disseminate a finished intelligence report derived from a technical source rather than a human source.

My operation was the first in the Latin American Division to provide information from a technical operation that was disseminated into an intelligence report. The report contained the plans of OMITTED to establish new official installations throughout Latin America. Generally, technical operations provide information that is used for security purposes. Seldom do technical operations provide data that is disseminated to the Intelligence Community.

I achieved significant accomplishments as a Case Officer in Latin America while at this post, but on the down side, Joe Lee relentlessly made the assignment really challenging. I led and directed Agency resources, especially foreign agents who provided me with access to Counter Intelligence information, such as technical intercept operations. These operations required one to use hardware and instruments along with intercept techniques to make the activity successful. I became an expert at initiating and designing technical operations. Ultimately, I ran a robust network of agents including some agents who worked technical operations as well.

When I returned to Washington in June, 1974, I learned that Dave Atlee Phillips had placed the letter in which I complained to him of Lee's treatment of me in my personnel file. Phillips was born on October 31, 1922 Forth Worth Texas and died July 7, 1988. He attended William and Mary College and Texas Christian University. He worked as a Case Officer aka spy manager at the CIA for 25 years and received the CIA Career Intelligence Medal. In 1975 he founded the Association of Former Intelligence Officers (AFIO), an alumni association comprised of intelligence officers from all services. Phillips joined the CIA as a part-time agent in 1950 OMITTED, where he owned and edited "The South Pacific Mail", an English-language newspaper that circulated throughout South America and several islands in the Pacific. He became a full-time spy manager in 1954 and rose through the ranks to Chief of Station and eventually chief of all operations in the Western Hemisphere (C/WHD), serving primarily in Latin America including OMITTED, OMITTED, OMITTED, OMITTED.

Phillips also gave me something of a pep talk, strongly implying he would continue to be my advocate within the WH Division. However, he became tainted with the allegations that the CIA tried to assassinate Fidel Castro and resigned from the agency, so I lost an ally. Unfortunately for me, Phillips did not get a chance to follow through on his promise to help me and other Blacks in the Division. Regardless of the events surrounding Phillips, Headquarters chose me for a great assignment and I had a wonderful extracurricular job.

Exceeding my own earlier expectations, on returning to Headquarters in the summer of 1974, the WHD appointed me as the Chief of the Counter Intelligence Section in the Central American Branch of the Latin American Division. I assisted the field stations in tracking certain Central American Counter Intelligence cases in Central American countries and worldwide.

Chapter 8:

Adviser to DCIA's - Colby and Bush

I realized only long after I left the CIA and returned to government service in 1989, that I had been involved at every stage in what came to be called "transformation management." Several of my Agency experiences enabled me to be involved in transformation management even before the terms existed for such activities. Let me frame history and tell how I can write exactly how CIA changed from a segregated government organization to one that overcame traditional cultural and ethnic biases. Perhaps the most important event took place under my watch and I had a opportunity to participate and monitor the institutional changes.

The activities of the DCI's Equal Employment Opportunity (EEO) Panel, an agency management advisory group, enabled me to be a "change agent" before the term was conceived. Change management took place in the CIA prior to 1976 and I was one of the key change agents. These improvement assignments empowered people like me to make significant recommendations for change. A living organization like CIA has to remain flexible to grow and adapt to changing circumstances. For me, these transformative experiences definitely serve as models for doing organizational change and transformation management translates into all group work.

The Director's EEO Advisory Panel was a major organizational change experience. To my surprise after my tour in the Latin American

Country, when I returned to Headquarters in 1974, I learned that Director William E. Colby had made a serious commitment to ending systemic ethnic and cultural discrimination in the CIA. Colby was the Director from September 4, 1973 to January 20, 1976. He believed that it was possible to create an American intelligence service that achieved the directive of President Richard Nixon for the Agency to actively enforce the EEO laws.

Colby wanted to implement an Agency Equal Employment Opportunity (EEO) program. During this time in history, I knew from the press that Colby was catching hell outside the Agency. However, he never faltered in responding to our support of him and in making himself available to the EEO Panel. The Agency and he were under investigation by three investigative Congressional bodies: Rockefeller Commission, the Church Committee, and the Pike Committees during the period from 1973 to 1976. This was all part of and due to the Congressional oversight aimed at curbing illegal CIA activity, disclosed to the public in 2007 as CIA's "Family Jewels." They included assassination attempts on foreign heads of state, the infamous MK Ultra mind control experiments, domestic covert action and other illegal actions, many of which took place before Colby's watch. Investigations concluded CIA violated its charter for 25 years, including surveillance and wiretapping of US journalists and dissidents. Discriminatory and domestic "dirty tricks" remain one of my "grinds," no matter which government agency is responsible.

The Rockefeller Commission

This Congressional advisory panel is named after Vice President Nelson Rockefeller who chaired it in 1974 during the Gerald Ford presidency. It performed an investigation of the CIA and it's in domestic spying against anti-Vietnam forces which became an issue because the CIA's charter restricted the Agency to foreign intelligence gathering. The Rockefeller Commission summed up the commission report:

"There are things that have been done which are in contradiction to the statutes, but in comparison to the total effort, they are not major."

However, there are serious concerns about the so-called "not major" finding. For instance:

1) It kept secret files on 10,000 American citizens.

2) It engaged in domestic wiretapping, breaking and entering, and opening people's mail.

3) It approved Mr. Nixon's "dirty tricks" plan, and abetted Howard Hunt's burglarizing.

All this was illegal, and its director, Richard Helms, lied about it to the Senate Foreign Relations Committee.

The CIA plotted to overthrow various governments; successfully in Iran and Guatemala, unsuccessfully in Cuba. It discussed assassinating Fidel Castro, with the Kennedy's approval, as Gen. Lansdale testified.

The CIA ran a program in Vietnam between 1967 and 1971, called Operation Phoenix, headed by then CIA director William Colby, who admitted over 20,000 Vietnamese civilians were executed without trial. That is a blood bath, by any definition. Further, that was after a secret paramilitary Covert Action intelligence operation took place as well even though CIA led by Colby was still involved. Ask the question how many years back did the actual secret paramilitary action start? Then put the pieces together if you can.

The Church Committee was created on February 19, 1975 led by Democrat Idaho Senator, Frank Church. It investigated the "skeletons" in the CIA closet, which included "kidnapping" of a KGB defector, wiretapping, illegal surveillance of journalists, dissidents and minorities, assassination attempts, warrant less entry, mail opening, and the notorious Project MK Ultra, which used unwitting human guinea pigs for behavioral modification, mind control, drug and other psycho-biological non-consensual human experiments.

While the Church Committee centered its attention on the more sensational charges of illegal activities by the CIA and other components of the IC, the Pike Committee set about examining the CIA's effectiveness and its costs to taxpayers.

Democratic Representative Otis Pike of New York headed the investigations of the Pike Committee. The Pike Committee closely examined the CIA's effectiveness and its costs to taxpayers. Unfortunately, Representative Pike, the committee, and its staff never developed a cooperative working relationship with the Agency or the Ford administration.

The committee soon was at odds with the CIA and the White House over questions of access to documents and information and the declassification of materials. Relations between the Agency and the Pike Committee became confrontational. CIA officials came to detest the committee and the efforts related to the investigation. Many observers maintained moreover, that Representative Pike was seeking to use the committee hearings to enhance his senatorial ambitions, and the committee staff, almost entirely young and anti-establishment, clashed with Agency and White House officials.

Just as he had done with the Rockefeller Commission and the Church Committee, DCI Colby promised his full cooperation to the Pike Committee. Colby, accompanied by Special Counsel Mitchell

Rogovin and Enno H. Knoche, Assistant to the Director, met with Pike and Congressman McClory, the ranking Republican on the committee, on 24 July 1975. At the meeting, Colby expressed his continuing belief that the committee would find that the main thrust of U.S. intelligence was "good, solid, and trustworthy."

Pike responded that he had no intention of destroying U.S. intelligence. What he wanted, he told Colby, was to build public and Congressional understanding and support for intelligence by "exposing" as much as possible of its nature without doing harm to proper intelligence activities. Pike indicated to Colby that he knew the investigation would cause "occasional conflict between us, but that a constructive approach by both sides should resolve it." Privately, Pike revealed that he believed the Agency was a "rogue elephant" out of control, as Senator Church had charged publicly. It needed to be restrained and major reporting reforms initiated.

According to CIA officer Richard Lehman, the Pike Committee staffers were "absolutely convinced that they were dealing with the devil incarnate." For Lehman, the Pike staff "came in loaded for bear."

Donald Gregg, the CIA officer responsible for coordinating Agency responses to the Pike Committee, remembered, "The months I spent with the Pike Committee made my tour in Vietnam seem like a picnic. I would vastly prefer to fight the Viet Cong than deal with a polemical investigation by a Congressional committee, which is what the Pike Committee [investigation] was." An underlying problem was the large cultural gap between officers trained in the early years of the Cold War and the young staffers of the anti-Vietnam and civil rights movements of the late 1960s and early 1970s.

Considering the pressure from these Congressional Committees on Colby, he still gave the EEO Advisory Panel adequate time. The Panel met with him and helped him get the EEO program installed in the agency. Colby selected Lewin (Lew) Warren to assist in organizing the EEO Panel. He apparently had been at it since 1972.

From my vantage point it was Lew Warren who was the person behind Colby's plan to re-engineer the Agency's culture and create a functioning Agency EEO program as required by the law.

One of the early steps in his strategy was to design and organize an EEO advisory panel. Fortunately I contacted Warren about the time he was organizing the Panel. I wanted to get first hand information on what the Agency was doing in EEO because the Chief of Station (COS) at my last post had made some disparaging remarks about the Headquarters EEO effort at one of the Station meetings. The COS laughed and joked about the Headquarters effort. Warren gave me the information and obviously determined that I was a good candidate for the Panel that he was organizing. The next thing I knew, I received a written invitation to participate.

I was named to the EEO Advisory Panel and quickly determined that Colby was in this for real. Warren wanted the mix on the panel to be from the four Agency Directorates, a mix of different ethnic groups and genders. I found it very helpful to get feedback from the only white male on the panel because his impressions tended to enable us to outmaneuver the other senior white male managers who received our recommendations. So our "token white" member of the Panel, Walter O'Brien, served the panel very well. The EEO Advisory Panel was empowered to challenge agency leaders and given authority to request actions for changing the ethnic mix. I later summarized many of the issues surrounding this period of my service in a letter to President George W. Bush, which I paraphrase here.

BEGINNING OF LETTER

Please consider our concerns and take the necessary actions about US government covert activities against African Americans to resolve

117

them, especially since the FBI Academy is unwilling to accept training from President Bush and us hasn't learned an important lesson from his father. I am writing this letter also to reveal some of the information I learned from former President Bush especially now that his son is President of the United States of America. We would like you to initiate a process improvement in the Intelligence Community to ensure corrective actions are taken to eradicate past, current and future injustices against US citizens because of government covert actions operations. I am offering this non-public process to you because I still believe you know what is correct and want to do the right thing.

The Central Intelligence Agency (CIA) employed me for 26 years from 1957 through 1984. When I left the Agency I was an intelligence officer and one of the few Agency Case Officers who had entered from Roosevelt High School in Washington DC, became an internal Career Trainee and successfully served abroad and at CIA Headquarters as an intelligence officer and communications security officer. As a historical footnote I am the only Agency case officer in the history of the Clandestine Services (CS) that served in Communications Security (COMSEC) after having completed significant services in the CS saw how it assisted me in recognizing the significance of the dual experiences. I use them to justify my statement that I can lead the CIA as well as the National Security Agency (NSA). I have now added the Small Business Administration (SBA) since I have demonstrated my aptitude in monitoring and enforcing the SBA Act on behalf of small business owners. In core competencies I know how to protect as well as collect information (steal) that others don't want to give up, especially telecommunications, communications and computer information.

Several significant events took place during my sojourn with the Agency that bears on my current concerns about injustice in government. Attached is an outline of the issues that have been taken place. From this outline I am sure that you can arrange corrective actions. However before I list these items let me further introduce myself and ensure that we all know are on the "same page."

When I was an adviser to your father at the CIA, he thanked me for my "great support of him" and his predecessor, William Colby. In your father's May 27, 1975 letter of appreciation to me concerning my service on the DCI's Equal Employment Opportunity Advisory Panel he wrote, "I understand that when it comes to pushing toward the objective of this important program, you speak from strength and have done much toward the identification of problems that we all seek solution to."

He closed the letter recognizing that I was a charter member of the Panel that Mr. Colby formally inaugurated on March 26, 1975.

END OF LETTER

Interestingly on April 1, 1975, Mr. Colby wrote a letter to heads of CIA offices advising them as follows: "I gave them the mandate to advise and counsel me and the Director, EEO on matters related to EEO, to evaluate EEO programs, and to identify problems and issues." He further stated that he also stressed to the Panel the importance of their responsibility and his eagerness to have the Agency move forward in "our EEO effort."

While on the EEO Advisory Panel, I networked extensively in the Agency. One very important contact I developed was a senior manager in the Personnel Division named Barbara Cooper. She was another Black, "who made it at CIA." I collaborated with her and obtained her guidance on the subject of personnel management to compensate for my limited personnel background. The issues in the Panel often dealt with personnel, so I wanted her expertise. We had several Administrative persons on the Panel, but none of them were from personnel.

Phillip Mason was elected the chair of the EEO Advisory Panel. Soon thereafter. He quickly worked his way into my graces and was gathering my knowledge on the Clandestine Services. Mason had come into the Agency as a GS-15, assigned to one of the executive senior staffs in budget and finance. He liked the idea of the Clandestine Services work even though he was a finance and budget type. He wanted to get a home base and he leaned toward the CS, so he eagerly learned about the CS from me during our service together.

Mason and I worked well together on the panel. I took the pro-active, confrontational position, and others chose roles close to their own personalities. We elected Mason as chair in part because of his maturity and management style. Phillip had statistics on where the senior-graded Blacks were located in the four Directorates. We met with the heads of the Directorates and determined their reasons for not having Black professionals in certain components; most reasons were not reasons at all but simply excuses.

The Advisory Panel started by interviewing the heads of each of the four Directorates. They all had different lies and excuses for not being able to find and hire Blacks. I had never seen white men lie and shiver so much. They had a myriad of excuses why they couldn't appoint or promote more Blacks to key positions. Some argued that Blacks couldn't pass the personnel evaluation battery tests. We produced an analysis that demonstrated how racially biased the current version was and suggested it be changed. We came up with names of qualified Blacks, but the heads of the Directorates said they didn't have slots for them.

When we reported to Mr. Colby, he indicated not having headroom was not an issue because he knew how the system worked. Colby let us know it was the senior management's excuse for not finding and hiring Blacks. We had many confrontations with senior Agency managers who appeared before the Advisory Panel. For example, Mr. Sara Stevens, Assistant Director of the Directorate of Science and Technology, told the morning staff meeting of top Agency managers that he had not been prepared for our meeting with him and that "the EEO Panel had kicked his behind."

On June 24, 1975, Mr. Colby in a commendation letter to me said that he had been deeply impressed with my dedication and professionalism during my three months on the panel. Colby wrote that I had effectively defined areas of interest and carried out projects and programs in fulfillment of the mission. Some of my friends scoffed and said that Colby probably wrote the same thing about a lot of people. I said, "Yeah, but I got the letter in which he wrote it about me. Where is yours?"

I use the comments from Colby about me to underscore an understanding of my propensity to get involved in issues of other people and organizations. This aspect of my personality really takes hold in a more meaningful manner after I leave the Agency. I call this trait of involvement a part of my mission on planet earth. I'm a born problem-solver and work out solutions for others most times better than if they had not had my assistance.

Interestingly, Mr. Colby in a letter dated April 1, 1975, also wrote to heads of CIA offices framing the scope of the EEO advisory committee. He stated, "I gave them the mandate to advise and counsel me and the Director, EEO, on matters related to EEO, to evaluate EEO programs, and to identify problems and issues." He further stated that he also stressed to the Panel the importance of our responsibility and his eagerness to have the Agency move forward in

121

"our EEO effort." I was in his presence more than five times. Since I have this talent, I was able to read his body language and concluded a little deeper meaning in his communications. I picked up the impression that Colby was serious and genuine about enabling the CIA to nurture a true "American Intelligence" service. Unfortunately, what I was not able to read or to know at that time is what I know today about the true intent of EEO in the grand scheme of double dealing in American culture. I think Colby, Bush and I, like others, have been unwitting in what I call the EEO double cross.

George Herbert Walker Bush replaced Colby in 1976. Bush met with the EEO Advisory Panel, though his commitment was not as evident as Colby's. in spite of this, DCI Bush supported the activities of the EEO Advisory Panel but made his decisions based on the "political ramifications" of any recommendation. DCI Bush was a member of the Yale secret society Order of Skull and Bones, which has produced an astounding number of CIA professionals who have sworn an allegiance to one another before entering the Agency. They stick together as a clique within CIA. Gaddis Smith, a history professor at Yale, said, "Yale has influenced the Central Intelligence Agency more than any other university, giving the CIA the atmosphere of a class reunion." And "Bonesman" have been foremost among the "spooks" building the CIA's "haunted house." You might call them "a culture within a culture" within the CIA.

The CIA and all other United States intelligence agencies still have a poor minority hiring record (14.1 percent are minority workers compared with 27 percent for the entire Federal government), however, progress has been made since I was among the active clandestine cadre. I have heard that at one time there were as many as 16 Senior Executive Service (SES) slots held by Blacks. The SES is the highest-level management leaders in the federal government. Anyone above a GS-15 is in this exclusive leadership group.

When I joined the Agency in 1957, there was only one Black Case Officer and of course he was not a SES. In 1976, when I was on the Panel and an advisor to DCI Bush, Mr. Bush wrote a letter dated May 27, 1976 that thanked me for my "great support of him and his predecessor," William Colby. He also stated in the letter that "I understand that when it comes to pushing toward the objective of this important program, you speak from strength and have done much toward the identification of problems that we all seek solutions to." Mr. Bush further recognized me as a charter member of the Panel that Mr. Colby formally inaugurated on March 26, 1975. With this type of management backing, I was able to position myself for some extraordinary success.

Chapter 9:

Assignment in Communications Security (COMSEC)

A few months after leaving the DCI's EEO Advisory Panel in 1976, I landed a significant position in a Directorate different than the DO. CIA management assigned me to the Office of Communications of the Directorate of Administration (DA) where I began as a Communications Security (COMSEC) Officer in the COMSEC Division. This assignment enabled me again to become a "first" as a pathfinder in the technical maze of CIA's administration and communications management. I became the first seasoned Spy Manager to pursue a senior management position in COMSEC and desegregated the management as well. Although there were Africans born in the USA already in the OC as communicators, the power structure in OC did not recognize the communicators as managers, so I gladly accepted the role to desegregate management in the COMSEC Division.

In COMSEC, I participated in and led quality teams that made significant recommendations to CIA senior management, including DCI Stansfield Turner. Once again I found myself serving as a change agent. My recurrent advisory role to the DCIs proved to be one hell of an educational experience. The teams of experts, today called Subject Matter Experts (SME), worked across OC organizational lines. We were tasked with designing and delivering significant solutions to issues within an organization like CIA in telecommunications and information management. Since I was one of the key movers and shakers on the team, I even had the audacity to present the DCI with a recommendation concerning counter intelligence technical capabilities of the Intelligence Community (IC).

I consider the EEO Advisory Panel experience with the DCIs Colby and Bush as quality team experiences. While the EEO Panel focused on a niche market in the Agency, we were still able to cross the traditional pipelines and stove pipes in agency organization. We accomplished some very exciting transitional changes because the DCIs backed the Panel and implemented our recommendations on changing the ways the CIA handled both diversity and business as usual.

Solving issues and problems in CIA's Office of Communications required an entirely different leadership strategy. The Quality Teams met and turned quality reports over to DCI Admiral Standsfield Turner. These unique leadership experiences were first-hand opportunities for me to meet and interact with yet another agency DCI. The quality teams were composed of communications personnel and we focused on quality management issues.

During my six years in COMSEC, I performed Information Assurance (IA) duties as defined in DOD Directive 3600.1: Information operations (IO) protect and defend information and information systems by ensuring their availability, integrity, authentication, confidentiality, and non-repudiation. The duties also included leading agency teams to restore information systems by incorporating protection, detection, and reaction capabilities. At the Agency, I also included information systems security (INFOSEC). INFOSEC is defined in the National Security Systems Issuances - NSTISSI 4009, which contains information about the protection of information systems against unauthorized access to or modification of information, whether in storage, manipulation, processing or transit, and against the denial of service to authorized users, including those measures necessary to detect, document, and counter such threats. I also conducted technical and non-technical security assessments of U.S. military, Department of State and CIA Information Technologies to determine the residual risk of operations.

I had additional experiences that pertain to the Defense Information Systems Agency (DISA) requirements. The Department of Defense (DOD) and other Federal Agency information travels extensively in electronic form on commercial infrastructures as well as on government owned and operated systems. Therefore, the information used for DOD and national security information is the same used for other types of electronically transmitted information.

My Agency experience pre-dated The Presidential Commission on Critical Infrastructure Protection. However, I was responsible for the Intelligence Community (IC) and closed some of the weaknesses that existed in intra-inter-agency counter technical and counter threat assessments. These very improvements led to solutions in Information Assurance that was eventually promulgated in the Presidential Decision Directive-63 (PDD-63) that serves as a framework for addressing critical infrastructure vulnerability issues.

Many of the personnel in the CIA are not under cover so their names can safely appear in public documents identifying them as CIA employees without causing any difficulty; Ms. Sharon Parish is one such individual. Her contributions helped me do well when I performed as a change management agent in the CIA before such a concept existed. This quality team, which I led from the Office of Communications, included several key people who enabled us to perform well. Ms. Parish, who then was the secretary to the Chief of Communications Security (COMSEC), served on our quality team. Larry Myers, then Chief of COMSEC and I discussed the addition of

Sharon to the team because we agreed that she would enable us to prepare well-organized quality reports with great content and style.

In 1976 we researched and wrote one quality report that set out a detailed plan for combining information management and telecommunications. This report was well received by Admiral Turner and later the agency followed forward, combining information management and telecommunications, securely regulating all communications and data management into one major component.

Our second report clearly identified the failure of the U.S. Government to research and develop a way to accurately assess technical Threat and Vulnerability issues in the Intelligence Community -- electronic vulnerability issues. Electronic security remains a crucial issue to this day. Fortunately, while I was leading this quality team, we had the opportunity to improve the way the entire agency protected communications systems, worldwide.

Thus a primary vulnerability issue was identified and resolved using arguments I based on traditional human counter-intelligence techniques. Just think. if I had not been on the team at that time in history the U.S. government would not have saved millions of dollars in subsequently designing and implementing COMSEC strategic security plans. It was odd that I was the only person on the team with a combination of technical and Counter Intelligence skills; it led the quality team and our products to become valuable versus previously-ignored countermeasure solutions. As usual, I brought my unique point of view to bear on the situation. Colloquially, this is called "out of the box" thinking since conformity and lack of innovation plague bureaucracies stuck in the status quo. These creative management techniques are now common, but such was not the case at the time.

We came up with certain innovative concepts challenging to the old order. It was not always cost-effective to spend money protecting

U.S. electronic vulnerability even when the adversaries knew theoretically how to exploit those vulnerabilities. Capability did not mean they could or would engage at that level. We simply needed to know what they were doing and not doing. We were able to demonstrate and prove we could still provide enough security protection when we had adequate agent information informing us of the capabilities and activities of the adversary. When we knew what they realistically could and could not do, we could exploit the weaknesses and oversights of the adversary, rather than striving for unrealistic and costly protections of our own vulnerabilities.

In one exercise, we combined technical vulnerability studies with traditional human counter intelligence techniques. The net result was the United States government saved lots of money. It no longer had to use funds to protect vulnerabilities that we clearly knew foreign adversaries did not have the ability to attack. Our report described this issue as "woefully neglected." We learned how to limit our exposure. Admiral Turner accepted the report. During our meeting with him, he asked his key staff person whether the description was accurate. Rusty responded affirmatively to our characterization of the communications security situation as a calculated risk. Risk assessment and management, in general, became another of my specialties.

For about two years after that meeting with Admiral Turner, I was amazed to see how the very project and program officers responsible for original shortcomings in the Intelligence Community and in the Agency wrote position papers avoiding responsibility for the state of affairs on both issues. The Director's office shared the reports with me. In the end, both weaknesses in telecommunications and information security were buttoned up. I did not receive any Agency recognition for providing the ideas and recommendations for re-engineering information management and technical counter-intelligence. It was just part of my job, but I was personally pleased to have done so, since it served our nation's common goal of state security.

We changed the regulations so that communicators were treated equally like the Case Officers when they wanted to marry a foreigner. I shared this news during my inspection visits to the communications facilities so the communicators learned that they could marry without having to quit which was the old policy.

OC types were amazed at my knowledge of 'Commo' even though I was a Case Officer and in their mind's eye, I was not supposed to know much about information assurance and security of telecommunications.

When I returned from my last tour with the CIA in 1981, two things happened that are pertinent to my re-inventing myself and seeking ways to get back into spy management.

I went to work as a Headquarters field support unit of COMSEC and remained in the Office of Communications. My superior, Red Neck, was determined to cast aspersions on my work. I irritated him by questioning him about the requirements of specific assignments so that I would know what he expected of me. Then I would follow the instructions to the letter, limiting the possibilities for criticism.

I had the opportunity to be interviewed by a professor from Howard University, Ms. Brenda Clement Frazier, who had the Agency internship assignment to interview the CIA Black Case Officers so I welcomed the opportunity. At that time in 1982, I was still in the Directorate of Administration's Office of Communications working in Communications Security (COMSEC) Division. A young lady conducting the interviews also happened to be a professor of Spanish. When she approached me, I quickly agreed to meet her in the office that I shared with three other COMSEC Officers. We handled headquarters duties supporting the CIA Communications Areas around the world. I had recently returned from Asia, so naturally my work supported the CIA Communications facilities in Asian countries. When the professor and I began the conversation I discovered she was a professor of Spanish, so I suggested that we do the interview in Spanish. She agreed and we had an animated exchange *en Espanol* while my office roommates looked on without having a ghost of an idea what we were saying. Wow what a session.

We discussed my Agency training as shown in the following table except for the years 1969 through 1970 and that was all CIA training; Career Training, Agency Administrative Procedures (Including Personnel, Procurement, and Other Activities) :

Date	Hours	Subject	School
1958	40	Information Management	CIA
1959	80	Records 1,2,3	CIA
1959	60	Security and Communications	USAF
1959	60	On-Line Cryptographic Systems	USAF
1959	320	Cryptography	USAF
1962	40	Off-Line Systems	CIA
1962	80	On-Line Systems	CIA

1966	40	Intelligence Agencies Name Check	CIA
1967	40	Conducting Counter Intelligence Operations	CIA
1972	40	Latin American Affairs	Department of State
1974	80	How to Conduct Performance Appraisals	CIA
1978	80	Health and Safety 1 and 2	CIA
1981	40	Asian Policy	Department of State

Chapter 10:

Desegregating Management In the DO's Arab Operations

My meeting and discussions with Professor Frazier Clements served as an important transition in my life from the DA/OC back to the DO. That is, I reconnected with the Directorate of Operations and desegregated the management in the Near East & Asia (NEA) Division which for the first time enabled me to work Arab countries and adversaries within a few short weeks after Professor Clements and I had talked. Please note that when I was telling my story to her up to 1981 I did not share my feelings with her of my wanting to return back to clandestine operations. The conversation with her made me nostalgic and I immediately called one of my godfathers, asking him to help me get back into the DO, as soon as possible. My original dream was calling me "home." In short, that's how I returned to operations fieldwork from administrative duties where I gained experience in Information Assurance (IA). My mentor arranged for me to meet Dan Webster, then Chief of the Libyan Branch. Within a very short time, the deal was cut for me to get back into the DO but this time in the NEA Division on the Libyan Branch. My work had now covered five continents: Europe, South America, North America, Asia, and now Africa. This was my first assignment involving Muslim culture, though I had a superficial awareness of the Nation of Islam (NOI), the Black Muslims. I always found other peoples' spirituality, or lack of it, of great interest. Libya's religious leanings or underpinnings were not an issue at the time. This was to be another adventure in risk assessment.

In 1982, the White House grew concerned that Qaddafi might orchestrate a strike against targets within the United States and asked whether Qaddafi could mount a successful assassination against the President of the United States. Yes, you guessed who in the CIA got the assignment -- "me." The U.S. government continually engaged in intelligence reporting on Libya so the Agency was asked to perform the specific assessment. My Top Secret Report that we called a "White Paper" landed on the desk of the President. I even had one conversation with one of the White House persons who assisted in the coordination and the delivery of the White Paper. With such a high profile assignment, I used multiple Intelligence Community (IC) resources to make the assessment. The process required the use of satellites (hi-tech) and human (no-tech) sources

To assess the "Libyan Show" as a veteran at Counter Intelligence expert, I gathered and developed reams of information on Qaddafi, who the United States had labeled an enemy of the state. I always considered him to be a threat that the United States had created using Covert Action intelligence operations; nevertheless, I had to perform my work as if Libya was consistently up to some harm to the United States and other countries. Unfortunately, that was the nature of the "Libyan Show" as it was called. In "Wag the Dog" style, it was a manufactured crisis, a contrived drama.

Also, I quickly realized that I was performing CI work against a USA created untrue image of certain government leaders like Qaddafi. That is, Libya was not as bad an adversary as the public profile and the hard facts were indicating. My unique enlightening experiences in the "Libyan Show" enabled me to have a very sober and memorable experience assessing Libyan President Muammar al Qaddafi. I prefer to say that the United States made him appear to be a greater threat than he was. It allowed the US leaders to do some militaristic "grandstanding," and demonstrations of force – what the military calls "battle rattle."

I had the opportunity to direct multiple Agency resources, both human intelligence (HUMINT) and signals intelligence (SIGINT). The latter collection required my working closely with Agency intelligence officers in the Directorate of Science and Technology (DS&T). They actually directed Agency SIGINT resources that augmented the HUMINT collection operations generally performed in the Clandestine Services or the Directorate of Operations (DO), where I began in 1957, nearly 30 years before.

This was a challenging and exciting experience. I was amazed that I, who started out as a lowly Agency peon in the Records Integration Division of the DO as a still photographer, was responsible for developing a "White Paper" to help the President of the United States of America decide on future actions against Libya. Look at me. I'm running things! I'm the Head Negro in charge!

The CIA had assigned me to the Libyan Branch as Chief Counter Intelligence for Libya. Thus, I had to collect information and develop a secret report on Gaddafi at the expressed request of the White House. Because of this task and related experiences while being assigned to perform counter intelligence duties for the Agency's activities in monitoring Libya, I had the opportunity to learn a great deal about Gaddafi and the Libyan government from 1982-1984.

Soon, my supportive superior, Dan Webster, left to take a foreign post and my luck changed for the worse. There were some serious mistakes made by the Division. It seemed clear I was being set up to take the fall -- shit runs downstream and that is where I was standing.

I had achieved my objective and became a CIA Case Officer aka Spy Manager. My dream was realized. This experience in the Agency prepared me for the next phase of my life. My goals were shifting and I wanted to try my hand at doing business and becoming an international entrepreneur.

Earlier in my Agency experience, I probably would have been deceived into thinking I would be treated fairly. Officers in the Clandestine Services have good people skills so they can gain the confidences of colleagues and others they must influence, including the spies they recruit.

I had worked in Libya. My own paradigm is that the country of Libya is on the continent of Africa, but the Agency resources working against Libya where housed in the NEA Division. I did some digging and I found out that Libya was at one time in the Africa Division and technically I was not the first African American C/O or spy manager working against Libya. It may be safe to say Justice Arrow was the first Black Case Officer assigned to the Libyan Branch in roughly around 1957, when the Agency had Libya in the African Division. So in the early Agency they understood geography as it was. This destroyed my belief that I was the first Black Case Officer in the Libyan Branch, but technically I was still the "first" C/O to desegregate the NEA Division in 1982.

The history of Libya is not as many of us know it today. The country was never to be organized as one country as it is today. No one was promoting a united Libya. Their aim apparently was to encourage the creation of three separate states (Tripolitania, Cyrenaica, and Fezzan) which might subsequently, if they could, form a union among themselves, wrote the UN commission in Libya.

November 21, 1949; the United Nations" General Assembly voted to admit Libya

135

January 1, 1952; independence scheduled.

September 1, 1969; the military seized power in Libya and Captain Qaddafi took over Libya.

Let me take up the history building effort with my personal involvement in the Near East activities of the agency. In 1981 I returned to the States from Far East assignment and resumed leadership of an Agency quality team dealing with hi tech counter intelligence.

1981

Countering so-called Libyan terrorism and writing the White paper to the White House OMITTED, OMITTED, OMITTED, OMITTED were the high points of my assignment in the "Libyan Show".

During an operation abroad, I was the Headquarters point of contact for a fast developing critical intelligence situation. OMITTED, OMITTED. OMITTED, OMITTED, OMITTED. Now remember, I was the sole person in the CIA who was the expert on the Libyan Intelligence Service. Please excuse me for making it appear that the Libyan Intelligence Service was that sophisticated.

Thus, when the developments came about, I decided I did not want or need to get out of my bed and go from Washington DC to Headquarters in the middle of the night because there was a night action cable for me to handle. I re-invented how the Case Officer wrote and sent his message to Headquarters. Remember that I know how Commo worked and I knew how one performs abroad as a Case Officer. So I recommended, and the DO agreed, the Case Officer could write the message as if it was going through CIA communications without the Headquarters Case Officer – me -- having to sterilize it before going to the Intelligence Community. In short, everyone agreed and so it was done.

Sorry, the full details of this so-called Libyan intelligence story remain for another story I plan to tell, but I had to share this event because transformation management is a topic dear to my heart. In my cultural studies, I learned that Blacks had invented and improved their environment out of the necessity to reduce work for themselves. And so did I by re-inventing the handling of material written in the field so it could by-pass Headquarters processing in both the Office of Communications as well as the DO.

Knowing this tidbit raises questions around so-called stories about CIA 'not being able to deliver sensitive information fast enough to the Intelligence Community.' That, too, is for a future book and it is not relevant to my story now. However, I have plenty to say about what is true about what goes on in the Intelligence Community and what does not. My expertise was in ensuring rapid dissemination of information in critical and fast moving environments.

Here is another anomaly that I enjoy talking about. By using a "Nubian mind," I put events into a genuine historical perspective while removing the European spin that places Libya not on the African continent but in some place in the so-called Middle East. Both in Agency parlance as well as in the public eye, this anomaly takes place. Muslim countries are lumped together. The education system in intelligence denies the known facts of geographic positioning, considering Libya as a Middle Eastern, rather than an African country. Libya is not typically African so many don't realize it is on the African continent. Few bother asking, "Just where is Libya?" but accept the perception and terminologies that exist. In reality, we should question certain terms that wrongly define a situation.

Even in the CIA, the Agency perpetrated the mis-perception, positioning Libya in the Near East and Asian (NEA) Division, versus the Africa Division. Given this one example of flawed thinking and misinformation, I think you will understand when I point out that we live in a "cultural illusion." What we know is cached differently from the reality of the facts; the perception is different from the reality. The distortion is deliberate, the result of an agenda. Most of us just accept the information as truth for some unknown reason and go on with our daily affairs without challenging the validity or accuracy of the information.

While I am dealing with the African nature of Libya, let me also share with you how I got the notion I was really the first Black Case Officer in the NEA Division. Technically, I was, but not in reality. Eventually I met and debriefed Justice Arrow about his past service, especially since he was as far as we know either the first or one of the first Black Case Officers. It is safe to say he was the first Black Case Officer who was an external. Justice Arrow was assigned to the Libyan Branch in 1957 or there about, but then the Agency had Libya in the African Division. So in the early Agency they understood geography as it was. So it was confirmed that, technically, I was still the "first" to desegregate the NEA Division in 1982.

As a veteran of countering any intelligence operation, I gathered and developed reams of information on Gaddafi, who the United States had labeled as an "enemy of the state." I always considered him to be a threat that the United States had created using Covert Action intelligence operations. In other words Libya and Gaddafi were "boogey men" created by foreign dirty tricks of the USA. Nevertheless, I had to perform my work as if Libya was consistently making plans and making effort to do some harm to the United States and other countries. Unfortunately, that was the nature of the "Libyan Show" as it was called. In "Wag the Dog" style, it was a manufactured crisis, a contrived drama. Some may disagree but remember that I had the most intimate and best view to draw my conclusion from.

Soon, my supportive superior, Mr. Peepers, left to take a foreign post and my luck changed for the worse. There were some serious mistakes made by the Division. It seemed clear I was being set up to take the fall -- shit runs downstream and that is where I was standing. Earlier in my career, I probably would have been deceived into thinking I would be treated fairly. Officers in the Clandestine Services have good people skills so they can gain the confidences of colleagues and others they must influence, including the spies they recruit.

The nature of the Agency business, especially CA had some impact on my desire to leave the Agency, but the challenge of an international business was by far more exciting since I had achieved my dream to become a spy. I had learned how easily the good ole boys can cast someone off when it seems required by the task at hand. Realizing this, I was quite open to an opportunity to leave the agency. The expected challenge for international work as an entrepreneur was the main reason for leaving. The other is that I had achieved my objective and became an intelligence officer. My dream was realized. This experience in the Agency prepared me for the next phase of my life. That was, I wanted to try my hand at doing business and becoming an international entrepreneur. I left the CIA in January 1984.

These were two significant highlights of my tour in the "Libyan Show".

With the help from my buddy/godfather who I had met in the pool when I first joined the agency, OMITTED, we made the switch. Then a Case Officer in the NE Division, OMITTED facilitated my return to the DO.

I told Jeffrey that Hornet was the guy who educated me on the oligarchy and supremacy way back in 1950's. Now he facilitated the Agency placing me in the Near East Division. I told Jeffrey that it made me the first Black Case Officer in the division. Yes there had been other Blacks both male and female in the Division they were not Case Officers. One of my fellow case officers who got into NE after me shared a significant comment with me some years later. Philco Smart and I had been on the Director's EEO Advisory Panel and he said, "Mike you should have had the Division position as the Executive Officer and not merely a counter intelligence chief ." Jeff and I agreed that if that had happened in 1981 I would have been GS-15 or better and number 4 or 5 in the Division. No way at the time. I was fortunate to be a first genuine intelligence officer in the Division and a GS-12.

Hornet hooked me up with Mr. Dan Webster, Chief of the Libyan Branch/Station. At the time, I was thankful because I had no reference to compare my position. It turned out that I was the first Black professional to be assigned there and no one ever with my skill sets had been assigned in the Libya Station where the show was Covert Action versus Counter Intelligence. Though people were cordial enough, it was clear that I was not going to be cut in on the good assignments. If I wasn't going to be cut in on the good deals, I was going to take what I felt was mine. I muscled my way into an assignment involving Libya.

Though we didn't come right out and state it, the Libyan Branch operated like a Station in part because the Libyan government rejected any US diplomatic relations. So the concept of a Station to focus on a situation partially was conceived in 1982 when I was in the "Libyan Show," as we called it.

Some of us still maintain that the United States of America depends too much on doing Covert Action intelligence operations over the use of other traditional foreign intelligence and counter intelligence types of operations. During the last 100 years, the United States continues to create bogeymen and strengthen the US military industrial complex versus using more face to face, dialogue to dialogue negotiated understandings

Chapter 11:

Empowered and Enfranchised

Closing my memoirs is difficult because I wanted to continue the story beyond 1984 when I left the Agency. As you remember I started my story while I was riding in a limousine to and from BET on September 12, 2001, the day after 9/11. Naturally, my exciting life continued unfolding after I quit the CIA in 1984. With many exciting adventures and enlightenments remaining, I decided to write more stories in "The Dark Operative Series" (DO Series). Henceforth that is where you find these stories fictionalized in future stories from the DO Series.

I have described my three life passions in this memoir: Rose, my wife, my mother Ella's CIA and the CIA. Both women in my life inspired me through my growth as 26-year CIA employee, where I achieved my dream as a CIA spy manager. Most of all, I know without doubt that I am empowered and enfranchised because of them and their guidance and support then and even in my life now. I am using these three concepts to make some more points.

I have grown as a person from my experiences with Neuro-linguistic Programming (NLP) and now I am a practitioner of the Law of Deliberate Creation (LDC). I decided to also include some references for NLP found at the Web Site:
http://www.neurolinguisticprogramming.com/.

Also this You Tube address on LDC will give a little more insight: http://www.youtube.com/watch?v=BpN1BIMJ36w.

Yes, I am bringing useful transformational mind exercises into my story because I have incorporated these phenomenal concepts as practices in my life today, as my story continues.

I promised to remain focused in writing my autobiography, *Black Man In The CIA*. That challenge made me discern the appropriate close for the book in the first in a series of the Dark Operative Series (DO Series). As many of you probably noticed, I am a philosopher and visionary, so I look forward to sharing much of my thinking in future stories. Handing down years of stories about progress in building this country is important, personally and collectively. Unfortunately, many of us are just beginning to realize how the descendents of stolen people continue paving the way for human and civil rights in the United States and abroad. For me, achieving justice, peace and righteousness are end results that are right here, right now, if we simply claim them. How about you? Too many people with African heritage gave much to this country. I will not give up nor fail at making the United States a place for true justice. Anyone with me?

I wanted to use this Epilogue to reveal my discovery that I am an advocate for justice, righteousness and peace perhaps more than that is that even though the events in my story cover the CIA Cold War years, the story also documents CIA shift from a plantation mentality to a federal agency moving towards desegregation in the entire Agency and especially in the Clandestine Service (CS). In retrospect I had an opportunity to participate and now document many of the events that make the Agency a strong advocate for an American intelligence service.

Since I decided to end the philosophizing by setting the stage for my future writings, I could not leave my story without drilling down into my life and recognizing that I am O.K. and that I am truly a "drum major" as Dr. King, Jr. said. I am "living the dream," demonstrating it before and during my tenure at the CIA. Because this advocacy role is an underlying aspect of my personality, I find it very hard to first conceive and then to accept the notion that my United States government has some issues that need radical re-visioning. It has been hard to accept the notion that my government has performed trickery and duplicity on the citizens of the nation similar to the way the government has performed Covert Action (CA) in the international arena.

Fortunately, during these last 25 years, I have increased my core competency talents, knowing I can lead both the Central Intelligence and the National Security Agencies (CIA and NSA) toward better solutions. I developed a third core competency leading the Small Business Administration (SBA). It is really exciting for me to state my qualifications and watch people react when I ask them what part of my service they would like to hire or challenge. Yes, I have the gall and audacity to know I can perform at much higher levels than most people because I am experienced at meeting many challenges. Fortunately, my mission on planet earth as an advocate and "drum major" for justice, righteousness and peace demonstrate my gifts and capacities.

My associates have challenged me because I tend to nitpick about certain words and their usage. It is amazing that a concept like "racism" exists. Since there is only one human race on the planet, how can there be any conflicts? It is more appropriate to discuss "discrimination" rooted in culture and ethnicity. Since I object to living under the conceptual illusion that there are races of people on planet earth, I don't use the word "race" nor any words related to the linguistic fallacy. I hope you eliminate it as well. That led to my objection to the use of term "racism." Compromising, I do agree with the use of the term "institutional racism" because that exists.

Remember, if a concept doesn't exist the use of even part of the word in a term casts doubt on the word in my paradigm. These loaded "buzzwords" usually serve hidden agendas or the status quo.

Most definitions of empowerment revolve around the concept of enabling an individual to think, behave, take action, and control work and decision making in autonomous ways. I encourage us to take it one more step and see "Spirit" rather than ego as "the Doer." By knowing that we human beings are temples for the Spirit of God, we can access all the answers when we want and need them. So I encourage you to begin immediately thinking and listening to your emotions and the vibrations so you truly hear, feel and get empowered. "Enfranchisement" is when we have citizen rights and external privileges. I use that conceptual word mainly to counter the prevailing thoughts that humans are in various ways disenfranchised, meaning we lack something. I have good news for everyone -- when we claim the Spirit of God, we do not lack anything. Now that you realize the Spirit of God enables us humans to be empowered and enfranchised, please act accordingly.

I decided to elaborate on my worldview by listing my life accomplishments because that is my experiential evidence that God gave me my Spirit before I began this journey. Just think at the early age of 12 years old, I began passionately comprehending the value of my mother Ella's CIA employment. By the time I was 17, I found my second passion for Rose and the family we would raise together.

In 1963, CIA sent me, my wife Rose and three children overseas on our first assignment in the Far Northern Country (FNC). I happily completed the CIA's Career Training School(CTP) or "spy managers school" without a college degree in 1970. In 1971, I graduated from The American University in Washington D.C. with a Bachelor of Science Degree in Political Science, completing 11 courses while the government continued paying my salary while I went to school. Then, in 1972, the CIA sent me, my wife and five children abroad to a Latin American Country (LAC) where I served as a Spy Manager. After returning to Headquarters and while serving as Chief of Counter Intelligence for Central American Countries, I performed extra-curricular duties, advising the Directors of CIA. In 1976, the CIA assigned me to the Directorate of Administration where I served as a Communications Security (COMSEC) Officer in the Office of Communications. In 1984, I quit CIA after 26 years to become an entrepreneur working as an international food broker.

Most of all, I am happy to close my story by listing my experiences which demonstrate how I was empowered and enfranchised. Just think, some of us human beings don't know that we are members of the Global Majority and not a "minority" but a majority. Also remember, most people who identify with the Global Majority (GM) understand that people and governments use mind games and dirty tricks to confuse some of us, but not all of us. We can transform our attitudes at any point in life.

I often talk to our five adult children and eight grandchildren about relationships, given my belief that we are embodied as human beings with a "Spirit." The human body is a temple of Spirit, (see I Cor 3:16 and 6:19). I speak about my empowerment and enfranchisement whenever I get a chance. This enlightenment about empowerment and enfranchisement came to me while I was riding to Natasha's house after speaking on BET the day after 9/11. It really came to a head as I was completing this manuscript, ending the story by strongly restating this theme. Our adult children have begun to also benefit from my epiphanies while at the CIA and since I left in 1984. Hopefully, they are finding empowerment sooner than I did, benefiting from the experiences of their parents – Rose and myself. My memoirs have provided significant insights so you truly "think it so." Sooner rather than later, your human existence will catch up with your vision and/or thought. In my story you saw I got the vision of family that I wanted when I was a teenager. Rose joined my venture, helping me make my life a success as a man, husband and father – and productive citizen and spiritual being.

The greatest power I envision is co-creating life with the assistance of our Higher Power. Some call this "The Law of Deliberate Creation" (LDC), since the LDC can be performed to enhance what we want in life experiences. The Spirit that we each have is all knowing. However, the ego takes control of our mind at birth so it is up to us to give the Spirit the opportunity to lead. It is up to us to achieve our genuine Spiritual Gifts, Heart, Abilities, Personality and Experiences (SHAPE) given us before we are born. We are born with the "SHAPE" of a dual mission or ministry on planet Earth. Rick Warren's writings have significantly influenced me and I accept that before I was born that my Higher Power and my SHAPE were predetermined.

Thus, in the 26 years since I quit the CIA, I have significantly grown as a human being and definitely have a greater understanding of my Spiritual Powers. Yes, I know for sure that I didn't direct my life. My Spirit guided me all the way. I sincerely hope my story is inspirational for you in meeting your unique challenges and connecting with Spirit.

THE END

CPSIA information can be obtained
at www.ICGtesting.com
Printed in the USA
BVOW06s1837021017
496504BV00008B/46/P